D0842590

MASTERS of the KEYBOARD

LONDON : GEOFFREY CUMBERLEGE

OXFORD UNIVERSITY PRESS

Masters
OF THE
Keyboard

→≫ A BRIEF SURVEY OF PIANOFORTE MUSIC ≪←
By WILLI APEL

HARVARD UNIVERSITY PRESS
Cambridge, Massachusetts

1947

To URSULA

➤➤➤ PREFACE ◄◄◄

This book contains, with certain modifications and additions, the material of a series of eight lectures given in 1944 at the Lowell Institute of Boston under the title of "History of Music for the Pianoforte." It seemed advisable to replace this title by one more clearly indicative of the general character of this book, a book which, far from aiming at completeness and historical continuity, presents nothing more than a succession of landmarks, somewhat arbitrarily selected and loosely connected. It is the hope of the author that, in thus treating his subject, it has gained a certain freshness and spontaneity which will be appreciated by the musical amateurs to whom this book is primarily addressed.

This objective also accounts for a new method of presentation adopted in this book, that is, the inclusion of complete (or nearly complete) compositions, such as were played in the lectures. Novel though this procedure is, the author hardly feels that he should apologize for his veering away from tradition, but rather believes that he is taking a step long overdue. In fact, it is difficult to find a reason why to the present day musical amateurs should have been denied a privilege long enjoyed by students of the fine arts, where it is an established custom to include in books full reproductions of the works discussed in the text. Short examples, such as are usually found in books dealing with music, may suffice if the book is addressed to the scholar who knows where to find the full compositions, although even here they present at best a compromise. In the case of publications destined to be read by laymen, however, such a compromise actually becomes a deficiency.

On the other hand, it has not been deemed advisable to present the compositions with the editorial trappings, such as fingerings, legato and staccato signs, dynamic marks, and tempo indications, which are usually found in modern reprints of early compositions, particularly those of Johann Sebastian Bach. Although these additions may be of some help to the uninitiated performer, they nevertheless constitute a falsification of the original text, all the more since he is usually led to believe that they are authentic.

The completion of a comprehensive and scholarly study of the History of Early Keyboard Music is, at present, one of the main occupations of the author who, in two or three years, hopes to finish a project on which he has worked intermittently for well over twenty years.

W. A.

⇶ CONTENTS ⬳

1. THE KEYBOARD INSTRUMENTS   1

2. THE LATE MIDDLE AGES: 1300–1500   20

3. THE RENAISSANCE: 1500–1600   35

4. THE EARLY BAROQUE PERIOD: 1600–1675   77

5. THE LATE BAROQUE PERIOD: 1675–1750   108

6. THE ROCOCO PERIOD: 1725–1775   156

7. CLASSICISM: 1770–1830   184

8. ROMANTICISM: 1830–1900   230

9. IMPRESSIONISM AND THE NEW MUSIC: 1900–1940   272

    NOTES   307

    SOURCES   311

    INDEX   319

MASTERS of the KEYBOARD

THE KEYBOARD INSTRUMENTS

LIKE THE VIOLIN CLEF and music staff, the keyboard, that familiar pattern of white and black, has become a musical symbol. Within the world of music it rules over a large realm second in importance only to that emblematized by the conductor's baton which, nevertheless, it surpasses by virtue of its much older tradition and its much greater variety of forms and styles.

Realizing this fact, one may well stop to ponder about the inner reason why the pianoforte and its forerunners should hold such a commanding position in the world of music. As a matter of fact, nothing more artificial and, in a way, unmusical exists among the musical instruments than those complicated contrivances consisting of numerous levers, joints, rockers, pivots, hammers, springs, and all the other gadgets which make up what is usually called a key. Here is a violinist: his instrument rests firmly on his body, and his fingers act in living contact with the oscillating strings and the sensitive strokes of the bow. Here is an oboist, holding his instrument between his hands and his lips, with his breath flowing uninterruptedly from his lungs through the pipe, while the lips vibrate in contact with the delicate reeds. And here is the pianist or the organist, both far removed from their strings or pipes, busy with depressing lifeless ivory plates which, by a cleverly devised system of remote control, transform his finger movements into sounds in a manner hardly less artificial than that which transforms the typist's finger movement into letters and words.

Evidently, this manner of making music by remote control would never have gained so strong a foothold unless there were advantages far outweighing its patent deficiencies. Which, then, are these advantages? Perhaps the most obvious is the extraordinary enlargement of the tonal resources put at the disposal of a single player. It is, briefly speaking, the eighty-four strings handled by the pianist in comparison with the four strings of the violinist, or the hundreds and thousands of pipes controlled by the organ player as compared with the one pipe of the oboe player. Small wonder that, with such means at their command, the pianist and the organist should have tried, not without a considerable degree of success, to emulate and even to rival the orchestra. Nevertheless, the mere size of the tonal apparatus is not the main reason for the superiority of the keyboard instruments. This appears clearly from a comparison of the pianoforte with the harp, an instrument which also has a great number of strings—in certain types approximately the same as the pianoforte—but which has no keyboard. Obviously, in this case no increase of the tonal resources is gained by the addition of the keyboard. What *is* gained, however, is a much easier and more natural manner of playing. This, in fact, appears to be the most fundamental advantage of the keyboard instruments. They possess a finger technique which is more "natural" than that of any other instrument, insofar as there is a high degree—indeed, the highest possible degree—of conformity between the playing apparatus and the normal position of the hand and fingers. One has only to think of the fingering for a scale as required on the pianoforte, the violin, and the oboe in order to realize the naturalness and basic simplicity of the keyboard technique. Nor is there any instrument on which the simultaneous use of both hands or the position of the fingers in chord playing so fully conforms with what the written appearance of the music suggests. Yet another advantage of the keyboard is the clear visual arrangement of the tones, identical for the different octaves, and, within each octave, possessed of a clear distinction between the seven fundamental tones of the diatonic scale and the five additional tones of the chromatic scale. It is this feature in particular which accounts for the superiority of the pianoforte as an instrument for teaching purposes and for demonstration. Thus, largeness of resources, naturalness of technique, and conformity between the playing mechanism and the musical notation combine to make the pianoforte the most important, most versatile, and most serviceable single instrument; and these qualities readily explain its dominating position, a position, which, one may think, is properly indicated by its imposing size and impressively designed contours.

The pianoforte is a comparatively recent instrument. Its basic principles were developed shortly after 1700, but it was not until about 1770 that it began to supersede its forerunners and that a repertory of music proper for it was formed. Music for the pianoforte, in the proper sense of the word, therefore does not begin much before the time when Haydn and Mozart wrote their sonatas. However, to interpret the term piano music in this strict sense would be rather pedantic. In fact, it would mean excluding from the pianist's repertory such standard works as Bach's *Well-tempered Clavier,* or his suites and those by Handel, the sonatas by Domenico Scarlatti, and numerous other compositions of this and earlier periods. All these compositions were written, not for the pianoforte, but for the harpsichord and the clavichord, instruments which, although similar to the pianoforte in their possession of a keyboard, differ widely from it in sound-production as well as in tone color. Nevertheless, their common feature, the keyboard, is important enough to make these differences appear somewhat negligible, at least from the standpoint of the practical pianist who, without hesitation and scruples, considers the keyboard compositions of Bach, Handel, and Scarlatti his property together with those of Beethoven, Chopin, and Brahms.

Certain musical scholars, naturally inclined toward a more rigid view, have questioned the validity of this attitude. They object to a fugue by Bach, a suite by Handel, a sonata by Scarlatti being played on the piano, maintaining that in doing so some of the most characteristic qualities of these works are destroyed. The historical basis of this view is unassailable. There is no denying the fact that the pianoforte was virtually unknown during the lifetime of these composers, and that none of them ever wrote any composition with this instrument in mind. However, it seems that the above argument is not exclusively based upon such historical facts, but is also influenced by a decidedly modernistic line of thought insofar as it places an overemphasis on the importance of tone colors. No doubt the development of the modern orchestra with its variety of instruments, each characterized by a special timbre, has made composers and listeners extremely conscious of these individual qualities—so conscious indeed that the mere thought of giving the part of, say an oboe to a clarinet or flute is tantamount to sacrilege. This notion, however, is a characteristic product of the recent development of music. The older masters were much more indifferent in this matter, being concerned with the structural aspect of music rather than with its color effects. It did not make such a difference to them whether a melody was played on a violin or a flute, and they did not consider that a composition gained or lost by being performed on the harpsichord instead of on the organ. Particularly in the case of the various keyboard instruments we have ample proof that they were considered interchangeable. Numerous music books of the sixteenth century include in their titles remarks such as *pour les orgues, espinettes et manicordions* (for organs, harpsichords, and clavichords) ; or *per arpichordi, clavicembali, spinette e manachordi* (for harpsichords, cembali, spinets, and clavichords) ; or, even more summarily, *d'ogni sorte di stromenti* (for any kind of instruments) .[1] In the seventeenth and eighteenth centuries the lines of demarcation became somewhat clearer, though not nearly so clear as the modern mind would like to have them. A famous case in point is Bach's *Well-tempered Clavier*, written in the years between 1720 and 1744. To the present day the question as to whether these forty-eight preludes and fugues were written for the harpsichord or the clavichord, or perhaps for both, or possibly some pieces for the former and others for the latter instrument, has remained unsolved. One might think that the style of writing would give a clue about the intended medium of performance, but an unbiased analysis from this point of view results in even greater ambiguity. There are certain preludes and fugues which clearly point to the harpsichord as their source of inspiration, while others may be more properly claimed for the clavichord. There are still others, however, for which the organ or, in some cases, a string quartet, would appear as the ideal medium, and in many instances one cannot help holding the rather unorthodox view that a performance on a modern pianoforte is just as satisfactory, perhaps even more so, than one on any of the older instruments.

This remark brings us to the crux of the whole problem concerning the use of the pianoforte for music earlier than its repertory proper. To put it squarely, the problem is one, not of the piano, but of the pianist. There are thousands of people who play Bach's suites or fugues on an instrument which Bach saw only once in his life. There is nothing basically wrong with this. Many of these people, however, play these pieces in a style utterly foreign to Bach's concepts, and this is an altogether different matter. I have heard Bach being played with the speed of a Chopin etude; with the dramatic sweep of a Beethoven sonata; with the thunderous bravura of a Liszt rhapsody; with the lyricism of a Brahms intermezzo; with the decadent refinement of a Debussy prelude; with the suave and slightly nauseating velvet touch so dear to many modern pianists—but very seldom with the clarity, moderation, objectivity, and sincerity which are the basic requirements for the rendition of old music. It is this style of playing much more than the use of any specific instrument which is decisive in this matter, and the main advantage of the old instruments would seem to be that they do not lend themselves to the refinements and extravagancies of virtuoso pianism.

It would be unfair to close this excursion without adding at the end that "grain of salt" which so frequently makes all the difference between right and wrong. Although I do not think that the use of old instruments is *the* answer to our problem, nothing could be farther from my intention than to depreciate their significance, or to minimize the role they are playing in those most praiseworthy endeavors to revive the music of the past. Listening to the old masterworks being played on a harpsichord, a clavichord, or a Baroque organ is, no doubt, a fascinating and most rewarding experience. Moreover, it is perhaps only through such experience that the modern pianist may obtain a clear insight into the style of these works, enabling him to render them properly on his instrument.

After these introductory remarks we may now turn to a brief study of the four instruments for which the music to be discussed in this book was written: the organ, the clavichord, the harpsichord, and the pianoforte.

The organ is by far the oldest of all keyboard instruments. The principle of its construction—that is, pipes blown by artificial wind and keys by which the wind is admitted and stopped—goes back to Greek antiquity. About 250 B.C. Ktesibios, a Greek engineer living in Alexandria, built an organ which has become known under the name *hydraulis.* This name, which is composed of the Greek words *hydor,* water, and *aulos,* pipe, has given rise to rather fantastic ideas about this instrument, namely that water flowed through the pipes, and in some mysterious way produced an equally mysterious sound. Actually, water played a rather subordinate part in this organ, serving in exactly the same capacity which is indicated in the modern term "hydraulic," in other words, as a means of communicating pressure provided by hand pumps. A clay model found in the ruins of Carthage and portions of an actual instrument recently discovered near Budapest have given full insight into the details of its construction. On the clay model, shown in Figure 1,* several of these details are clearly distinguishable: three ranks of pipes, each containing nineteen pipes of varying lengths but all of the same diameter; two lateral metal containers serving as pumps, above which the shoulder pieces of the pump handles can still be seen; a large central container in which there was a hydraulic bell immersed in water; and between the two side pumps the legs of the organist who seems to be sitting on a high seat.

The hydraulis acquired great popularity in Rome where it was used at the banquets of the noble and wealthy, and, particularly, to accom-

* From *Grove's Dictionary of Music and Musicians* (3rd edition). By permission of The Macmillan Company, publishers.

pany gladiator fights and acrobatic performances. The Jews adopted it under the name of *hardulis* or *magrepha*, and possibly used it in the Temple, though certainly not until shortly before the end of Israel's national existence. In the early Christian era organ building was cultivated mainly in the Byzantine Empire. An obelisk, erected by the

1. WATER ORGAN—*Carthage*

Emperor Theodosius (d. 393), shows a representation of an organ with bellows instead of the hydraulic mechanism used previously (Fig. 2).* In western Europe the earliest evidence of the organ dates from 757 A.D., when the Byzantine Emperor Copronymos sent one as a gift to the Frankish King Pippin. As a matter of fact, it seems that during the first thousand years of our era organs were considered a most fitting present among royalty, as were dwarfs or diamond-studded swords at a later time.

A very interesting representation of an early Frankish organ is

* From *Grove's Dictionary of Music and Musicians* (3rd edition). By permission of The Macmillan Company, publishers.

2. ORGAN—*Obelisk of Theodosius*

found in the famous Utrecht Psalter of about 800 A.D. (Fig. 3). It shows an organ of only eight pipes, two monks seated behind it, and four men working hard on the long beams connected with two large wind containers. The monks seem to be occupied with inciting and scolding the bellows-blowers rather than with playing, and one can-

3. ORGAN—*Utrecht Psalter*

not help feeling that the music resulting from this fight of six strong men against eight helpless organ pipes was far removed from liturgical dignity and devotion. The impression that the early western organs produced a crude and powerful sound is confirmed by a report about an instrument which was built about 980 A.D. in Winchester, England.[2] It had, we are told by the monk Wulstan, four hundred pipes and twenty-six bellows which were worked by seventy men "labouring with their arms, covered with perspiration, each inciting his companions to drive the wind up with all its strength, that the full-bosomed box may speak with its 400 pipes." The result of such efforts was overpowering rather than pleasant, judging from Wulstan's observation that "everyone stops his gaping ears with his hands, being in no wise able to draw near and bear the sound."

Fortunately, organ builders of the subsequent centuries turned away from these monstrosities, and cultivated smaller types, such as the portative and the positive organ. The portative organ was an instrument small enough to be carried by one or two men, and so was used for chamber music and for processions. One of the greatest composers of the fourteenth century, the Italian Francesco Landini, was famous for his playing on the portative organ or, as it was then called in Italy, the *organetto*. A miniature contained in the splendid manuscript in which most of his compositions are preserved [3] shows him playing this instrument. A most touching description of his playing is preserved in a well-known literary source of the period, Giovanni da Prato's *Paradiso degli Alberti*. Here we are told that Francesco was asked to play on the organetto to see if the singing of the birds would lessen or increase with his playing. At first "the birds became silent *quasi attoniti*" (as if stupefied) but soon they redoubled their singing and one nightingale came and perched on a branch over his head.

The positive organ of the Middle Ages was a stationary instrument of medium size, used mainly in churches. Jan van Eyck's famous painting from the altar of Ghent, showing an angel playing the positive organ, is reproduced here (Fig. 4). With typical fifteenth-century attention to detail, the great Flemish painter has given a most accurate picture of the instrument. A detail which is perhaps not noticed at first glance, but which is of particular interest, is the equal diameter of all the pipes. In order to understand the significance of this detail, it must first be noticed that the medieval organs had as yet no stops, that is to say, controlling devices which enable the organist to bring into play different sets of pipes each of which has an individual timbre. Van Eyck's organ shows two sets, or, to use the technical term, two ranks of pipes, and other organs of the period had three, but these were always played together, producing a single and invariable sound. Nevertheless, these organs did not sound as uniformly as, for instance,

4. ORGAN—*Van Eyck Altar of Ghent*

a single stop of the modern organ, and the reason for this is the equal diameter of all the pipes. This principle of construction, which is to be observed in the Carthaginian clay model as well as in all the medieval organs, is in direct opposition to the modern principle according to which the diameter varies in proportion to the length of the pipes or, to use the technical term, according to which all pipes are made to scale. It is easy to understand that all such pipes have the same acoustic properties, that is, the same selection and arrangement of overtones. As a result, they all have the same timbre, for instance, that of a flute if the scale (the ratio of width to length) is wide, or of a stringed

·10·

instrument if the scale is narrow. Conversely, the pipes of the medieval organ, having all the same diameter, vary from a narrow scale for the long pipes to a wide scale for the short pipes. Hence, their timbre varies from a String tone in the low registers to a Flute tone in the upper ranges. If, by way of comparison, we characterize the sound of the modern organ as consisting of numerous bands, each in a different color, then the medieval organ possesses only one band, but varying in color like the spectrum. The musical qualities of this acoustical spectrum are quite remarkable. The change from a very narrow to a rather wide scale produces accurate definition and acuteness in the low octaves, fullness of volume in the middle register, and a marked softness in the high range. Shortly before the war there was a movement in Germany to build positive organs of the medieval type, and it is to be hoped that these efforts are being continued, perhaps in this country.

This is not the place to enter into a detailed description of the ensuing history of the organ, leading from the late medieval, or Gothic organ, to the organ of the Renaissance and, finally, to the Baroque organ. Suffice it to say that, in the fifteenth century, the spectral band of the medieval organ was replaced by separate colors, that is, by different stops each with its individual and uniform timbre. These timbres, however, differed markedly from those found in modern organs and, on the whole, represented a much more satisfactory solution of the organ problem than those of the present day. In fact, no unbiased observer can help feeling that the modern organ, although equipped with all the achievements of modern science and technique, is a failure in its most important aspect, its sound; for its tone is just as dull and characterless in the soft registers, as it is oppressive and deafening in the loud ones. The registers of the old organs were entirely different: strongly individual, incisive, full of overtones, and occasionally harsh. Arnolt Schlick who, in 1511, wrote an important book on organ building, repeatedly uses the word *scharf schneidend*—sharply cutting—in order to characterize the stops he describes.

In the seventeenth century there developed a new type of organ,

5. HARPSICHORD

known as the Baroque organ, which retained the contrasting qualities of the Gothic organ, but in softer and lighter timbres. It combined "horizontal" individuality with "vertical" homogeneity, as did the organ music of the Baroque period, especially that of Bach. It is very gratifying to see that modern organ building is now turning back to this instrument in order to make possible the adequate rendition of the greatest organ music ever written.[4]

The stringed keyboard instruments, which we shall now briefly consider, are of three types, distinguished by the manner in which the strings are set in vibration. In the harpsichord (Fig. 5) the strings are plucked, as in the playing of the harp; in the clavichord (Fig. 6)

6. CLAVICHORD

they are made to sound by a sort of pressure-stroke, a method somewhat similar to that of a violinist merely "fingering" on a string; in the pianoforte they are struck by hammers.

The main part of the harpsichord action (Fig. 7) is the jack, a lengthy piece of wood which at the upper end bears a plectrum made from crow quills or from leather. The jack rests on the rear end of the

7. HARPSICHORD ACTION

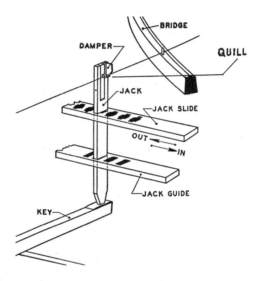

prolonged key which, on being depressed, causes the jack to jump up so that the plectrum plucks the string. To each key belong several jacks which produce a slightly different timbre, owing to the different material of the plectrum. There are also different strings to each key which produce lower or higher octaves. The jacks are held in position by two long boards with rectangular cuts, the jack guide and the jack slide. The latter can be moved sidewards by means of a pedal or a hand stop, thus bringing one or several of the plectrums into contact with the strings.

The action of the clavichord is much simpler (Fig. 8). To the rear end of each key there is fastened a small brass wedge in the shape of a

·14·

T, called the tangent. Upon depressing the key the tangent is pressed from below against the string.

The sound of the harpsichord is incisive and brilliant. It has a silvery twang which immediately attracts the attention of the listener. From the modern viewpoint its greatest deficiency is its inability to produce gradation of sound by lighter and stronger touch, as is possible with the pianoforte. To some extent this deficiency is made up for by the different stops which permit a modest degree of registra-

8. CLAVICHORD ACTION

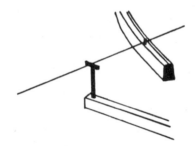

tion, so that one section of a piece can be made to sound piano, the other forte. In both respects the harpsichord is similar to the organ. Another feature derived from organ building is the presence of two manuals, which can be used either in alternation or simultaneously— one for the right, the other for the left hand. Thus, a two-part composition (for example, an invention by Bach) can be played in a number of different ways: both parts on the lower manual, or both on the upper, or one on the lower and the other on the upper, and so on. Furthermore, for each manual a variety of timbres are usually available; for example, on the lower manual there are two different eight-foot stops (one with plectrums made from leather, the other from quills), to which can be added (by means of hand stops or pedals) a four-foot stop, sounding an octave above normal, or a sixteen-foot stop, sounding an octave below normal.

It appears, then, that the harpsichord possesses a considerable amount of variation in sound. However, the importance of these devices should not be overestimated. In many compositions by Bach and other Baroque composers there is little if any chance to use them; the preludes and fugues from the *Well-tempered Clavier* are examples in point. In other compositions, for instance in Bach's *Italian Concerto,* the contrast between sections in forte and others in piano is an essential feature of style and form. On the whole, however, there is little doubt that Bach and his contemporaries used the registers of the harpsichord to a lesser extent than do most modern harpsichord players. A compelling reason for this is the fact that in the old harpsichord the change of registers was made exclusively by hand stops, not by pedals such as are used in most of the modern reproductions. This, of course, puts a definite limitation on the free and frequent change of stops.

The clavichord is an altogether different instrument from the harpsichord. In a certain respect it approaches the pianoforte since gradations of sound can be obtained by using a lighter or stronger touch. These nuances, however, are extremely slight since the whole dynamic range of the clavichord varies from a pianissimo quality to a mezzo-piano at the most. People who hear it for the first time are bound to be thoroughly disappointed even in their most modest expectations. They will wonder how anybody could ever have derived satisfaction from so tiny a sound. To demonstrate the clavichord before an audience of some size is practically impossible, because its sound carries over hardly more than a very small distance. This fact makes the instrument entirely unsuited for public performance. It is only by playing it with one's own hands that its remarkable qualities become apparent. Musicians from the sixteenth to the eighteenth centuries, particularly in Germany, deeply appreciated what was called the *beseelter Ton*—the soulful sound—of the clavichord. There is no other instrument which fosters so complete a union between the instrument and the hand, between the ear and the mind. Nor is there one which so fully rewards whoever is willing to listen to its enchanting sound.

The earliest mention of a stringed keyboard instrument is made in a letter of the Spanish King John of Aragon, written in 1367 and addressed to an envoy whom he requests to search for somebody able to play the *exaquir,* an instrument which he describes as *semblant d'orguens que sona ab cordes* (similar to the organ but sounding by strings). The same instrument is mentioned in various literary sources of the fifteenth century under names such as *eschaquier, eschiquier, chekker,* and as late as 1574 we find the *escacherium* listed among other keyboard instruments. Scholars disagree as to whether this was a clavichord or a harpsichord.[5] Both these types were known around 1400, as appears from a German poem of 1404, *Der Minne Regeln,* in which the *clavichordium* and the *clavicimbalum* are mentioned among the instruments of courtly love. Clavicimbalum is the original Latin name for the harpsichord, a name which survives to the present day in the Italian term *clavicembalo,* the German *Cembalo,* and the French *clavecin.*

The clavichord was fairly widely used during the sixteenth century. Various musical sources mention it in their titles, and many pictures show young ladies playing the clavichord with delicate fingers. These instruments were a great deal smaller and, consequently, even softer than those used in the eighteenth century. Frequently they were less than two feet in length, so that they could be placed on a table and carried along while traveling. Together with the lute, the clavichord represented in the sixteenth century what the upright piano is today, the favored instrument for unpretentious domestic music making. During the seventeenth century it was gradually put into eclipse by the harpsichord, except in Germany where it continued to be appreciated for its *beseelter Ton.* Shortly before the pianoforte emerged as a victorious rival, the clavichord found a most eloquent champion in Johann Sebastian Bach's son, Karl Philipp Emanuel Bach.

The harpsichord achieved its first triumph in England during the Elizabethan period. There it was known under the name "virginal," or "pair of virginals"—this perhaps with reference to the two manuals. The current interpretation of the name virginal as referring to the "maiden Queen Elizabeth" is clearly refuted by the fact that the name occurs as early as 1511, in a book of the German Sebastian Virdung.[6] Writers of the seventeenth and eighteenth centuries usually say that the instruments were so called because "virgins play on them." In the Baroque period, from about 1650 to 1750, the harpsichord rose to prominence particularly in France, where composers like Chambonnières, d'Anglebert, Couperin, and Rameau created a large repertory of typical harpsichord music. The German composers of this period usually preferred a less idiomatic style which was suited for the harpsichord, the clavichord, and the organ. Among the works of Bach there are only two which can unequivocally be assigned to the harpsichord; these are the *Italian Concerto* and the *Goldberg Variations*.

At the time when these compositions were written, experiments were already being made with another instrument which was to mark an epoch in music history: the pianoforte. The origin of the pianoforte or, at least, of its distinguishing device, the hammer action, is usually traced back to the activity of one Pantaleon Hebenstreit who in the first decades of the eighteenth century toured Europe as a virtuoso of the *pantalon*, a large dulcimer played with hammers, like the cimbalom of the Hungarian gypsies. In fact, one of the various "inventors" of the pianoforte, Gottlieb Schröter, admitted in 1717 that Hebenstreit's playing had inspired his invention of a hammer mechanism which, however primitive, made it possible to play *piano e forte*—soft and loud—on the harpsichord. Several years earlier, however, in 1709, a much more perfect hammer mechanism had been invented by Bartolommeo Christofori of Florence, very likely without any knowledge of Hebenstreit's pantalon. In fact, it was not until about 1770 that instruments of such a perfection as those by Cristofori were made again. There is no need of our going into a detailed description of the development leading from Cristofori's instruments to the pianofortes of the present day. Suffice it to mention some outstanding names: Gottfried Silbermann who built the instrument on which Bach played in 1747; John Brent of Philadelphia who built the first American pianoforte in 1774; John Broadwood of London who built the first grand piano in 1796 and also made Beethoven's favorite instrument; Sébastien Érard of Paris who, in 1821, greatly improved the action by the invention of the so-called double escapement; and Alpheus Babcock of Boston who, in 1825, made the first full cast-iron frame instead of the wooden frame used previously.

As might be expected, the pianoforte, during its emergence in the second half of the eighteenth century, was received with hostility as well as enthusiasm. The Germans, unwilling to give up their beloved clavichord, rejected it most persistently; the French remained sceptical; but the English adopted it whole-heartedly. The relative merits and demerits of the three keyboard instruments—harpsichord, clavichord, and pianoforte—were a matter of frequent and heated discussion. The French harpsichord and organ composer Balbastre exclaimed: "You toil in vain, this upstart will never replace the majestic harpsichord," and Voltaire, in a letter of 1774, referred to the piano as a "boilermaker's instrument" compared to the harpsichord. The German point of view is clearly expressed by the anonymous author of a *Musik Handbuch für das Jahr 1782* who in degrees of absolute excellence places the piano over the harpsichord but below the clavichord, for "though it has more light and shade than the former and can express more varied emotions, it still has no middle tints and lacks the refined details of beauty of the clavichord." Burney, with his typical frankness, states the English attitude in the following words: "There is no instrument so favourable to such frothy and unmeaning music than the harpsichord. . . I remember well in the early part of my life being a dupe to this kind of tinsel, this *poussière dans les yeux*. . . At length, on the arrival of the late Mr. Bach[7] and construction of pianofortes in this country, the performers on keyed instruments were obliged wholly to change their ground; and instead of surprising by the seeming labour and dexterity of execution, had the real and more useful difficulties of taste, expression, and light and shade, to encounter."

With such well-considered judgment the pianoforte was safely started on its road to success.

1300 — THE LATE MIDDLE AGES — 1500

AFTER THE CONSIDERATION of the different keyboard instruments our attention turns to the subject proper of this book: the study of the music performed on these instruments. Evidence of various kinds has enabled us to trace back the history of the organ to pre-Christian times, and to pursue with considerable accuracy its course of evolution, leading from Alexandria and Rome to Byzantium, England, and continental Europe. Naturally, we would like to know what music was played on the organ in these early times, but with regard to this question we find ourselves in complete darkness. No example of Greek organ music has come down to us, and, in fact, it is doubtful whether such music was ever recorded in written symbols, since much of the music of ancient times was either improvised or, if considered worthy of preservation, was handed down by memory, as was the case for a long time with the Homeric epics. A similar situation probably existed throughout the period of the early Christian organ. Here, indeed, circumstances were even less favorable, since prior to the eleventh century the organ was found in palaces rather than in churches and therefore was of little interest to the clerics who at that time were the only people capable of writing down music.

Our documented knowledge of keyboard music begins shortly after 1300. A manuscript of the British Museum, known as the Robertsbridge Codex,[8] contains the earliest organ compositions that have been preserved. These pieces are usually believed to be of English origin, but the evidence in support of this theory is rather external and inconclusive. More pertinent are certain intrinsic features, and these clearly point to Italy as the home country of the earliest known organ music. The most important of these clues are details of the notation in which the pieces are written. While these details are too technical to be explained here, it may be of interest to examine briefly the general principles of the notational system employed, especially since this system remained in use for the writing down of keyboard music through the end of the sixteenth century.

We notice in Figure 9 a staff of five lines on which notes are written forming a melody. With the aid of the clef sign at the beginning

9. ROBERTSBRIDGE CODEX—*Facsimile*

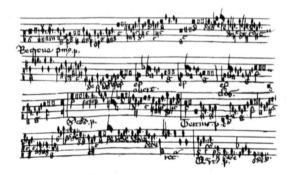

of the staff, denoting middle c, the pitches of the various notes can easily be determined. There remains the question of their rhythmic evaluation, and this presents a much more difficult problem. Suffice it to say that the principles involved here are exactly the same as those which were employed at the same time in Italian vocal music. Underneath these notes we find pitch letters, such as a, g, f, together with two other signs, one in the shape of the modern sharp, the other in the shape of an *s*. The pitch letters have their present-day meaning, indicating the tones a, g, f, and so on, while the sharp denotes our tone b, and the *s* stands for the Latin *sine* (i.e., "without"), thus indicating a rest. All these signs form a second melodic line, and the piece under consideration is, therefore, a composition in two voice parts. This

·21·

10. ROBERTSBRIDGE CODEX—*Organ Estampie*

method of indicating the lower tones not by notes, but by letters, is a characteristic feature of early keyboard notation. Figure 10 is a transcription in modern notation.[9]

Odd though this music sounds at first hearing, it has an archaic quality which is not without a certain charm. The main reason for its archaic sound is the extensive use of parallel fifths. This means that the lower voice moves parallel with the upper voice, a fifth below (Fig. 11).

11.

Even to the uninformed listener such sounds at once suggest a very early stage of music, but it would be wrong to assume that this style is characteristic of the fourteenth century, the time when this piece was written. Actually the writing in parallel fifths is typical of the earliest experiments in polyphonic music which took place in the ninth century, five hundred years before the date of the Robertsbridge pieces. It is very surprising to encounter this archaic style at a time when vocal music had progressed to much more advanced methods, involving the use of contrary motion, three-voice counterpoint, and complete rhythmic independence of the various voice parts. However, this is not the only example showing that keyboard music, in its infancy, was not only dependent on its elder brother, vocal music, but was also extremely slow in catching up with his steps.[10]

It may be noticed that our illustration shows only the beginning of the composition. The whole composition is rather extended—much too long to be reproduced here in its entirety—and belongs to a fairly common type of medieval instrumental music, namely, the *estampie*. The estampie originally was a dance or a dancing song, but our example represents a late stage of this form in which the original connotation is completely lost, and in which the estampie appears as an abstract type of music which occasionally shows certain traits of virtuosity. All the estampies, whether the earlier, more dance-like, or the later, more abstract examples, show a characteristic form consisting of various sections each of which is repeated, so that the scheme A A, B B, C C, and so on, results. These sections were called *punctus* (point), and the indications *primus punctus* (first point), *secundus punctus* (second point), *tertius punctus,* and *quartus punctus* can be seen in our facsimile. The word written at the beginning probably means Petrone, possibly with reference to the otherwise unknown composer of this organ piece.

In turning to the next source of keyboard music we have to take a jump of over one hundred years, owing to the complete lack of source

12. TABLATURE OF LUDOLF WILKIN—*Transcription*

material between about 1325 and 1432. Fortunately, the jump, though considerable in terms of time, turns out to be relatively small if gauged from the viewpoint of the development of organ style. The organ sources of the mid-fifteenth century contain some compositions which show very little advance over the primitive stage represented by the Robertsbridge Codex. Others—and these will be of greater interest to us—do show new traits, but even so their novelty is slight if compared with the extraordinary development which had taken place in vocal music. Under the Burgundian masters Dufay (1400?–1474) and Binchois (1400?–1460), vocal music had just reached one of the most glorious points of its entire history, and was passing into the hands of the great Flemish masters, Ockeghem (1430–1495) and

THE LATE MIDDLE AGES

Obrecht (1430?–1505). No traces of these momentous developments are found in the organ music of the period. At a time when vocal music was already exploring the full sonorities of four, occasionally even five and six, voice parts, organ music was still written in an archaic two-voice style. This style is illustrated by Figure 12, taken from a manuscript written in 1432 at Windsheim in northwestern Germany.

The backwardness of fifteenth-century organ music, if compared with the contemporary vocal music, is at least partially explained by the fact that all the extant organ pieces from this period were written in Germany, a country then far removed from the centers of musical art, such as the Burgundian court at Dijon, or the cathedral of Cambrai in northern France. But perhaps it was this very remoteness which enabled the German organists to develop, slowly and patiently, the resources of an instrument for which, at that time, competition with the highly advanced methods of vocal music might have proved a handicap rather than a stimulus. The first important result of these independent efforts was the establishment of a new musical form which by its very nature is foreign to the field of vocal music and proper to that of keyboard music, namely, the prelude. Figure 13 shows a page containing the earliest preludes that have been preserved, certainly also some of the earliest that were written.

This page is taken from a manuscript written in 1448 by Adam Ileborgh, rector of a monastery in Stendal, a town in North Germany which is known mainly as the place from which the French novelist, Henri Beyle, took his pseudonym, Stendhal. It may be of interest to mention that this manuscript is in the library of the Curtis Institute of Music in Philadelphia, and that it is probably the oldest and most valuable musical codex in the United States. At the top of the page there is an inscription which reads as follows: *Incipiunt praeludia diversarum notarum secundum modernum modum subtiliter et diligenter collecta cum mensuris diversis hic inferius annexis per fratrem Adam Ileborgh Anno Domini 1448 tempore sui rectoriatus in stendall*—"Here begin preludes in various keys [composed] in the mod-

·25·

ern style, cleverly and diligently collected, with diverse *mensurae* appended below, by brother Adam Ileborgh, in the year of our Lord 1448, during the time of his rectorate in Stendal." There follows the inscription for the first staff of music: *Sequitur praeambulum in C, et potest variari in d, f, g, a,* that is: "Here follows a prelude in the key of C, which can be transposed into the keys of D, F, G, and A."

The notation of this and the subsequent preludes is essentially the same as that of the Robertsbridge Codex. The upper part is written on a staff, while a lower part is indicated underneath by letters: c, g, d, f-sharp, c, g (the sharping is indicated by the loop attached to the letter f). The deciphering of this specimen is not without its difficulties, the main problem being that the lower line does not make sense if combined with the upper melody. The solution of this puzzle lies in the fact that the tones of the bass are to be played, not successively as indicated in Figure 14, but simultaneously in groups of two, as is

14.

shown in the final transcription (Fig. 15). Naturally, the question arises whether there is a reason for the curious manner of writing employed in the original. There is indeed: the lower part was to be

15. ILEBORGH—*Organ Prelude*

performed as a double pedal, with both feet playing simultaneously. Therefore the position of the two letters in each group corresponds to the position of the two feet, the first letter being played by the left foot, the second by the right.

The main problem presented by the upper part is that of its rhythm. Defying all attempts of evaluation in strict meter, this melody turns out to be an example of free rhythm, such as is rarely found in polyphonic music after 1200.[11] One may speculate whether it was this unusual style—certainly a short-lived innovation—to which Ileborgh refers by the words *secundum modernum modum*.

Much better known than Ileborgh is his contemporary Conrad Paumann (*c.* 1410–1473), who worked in southern Germany. Unlike many composers of old, Paumann is not a semi-legendary figure. His fame was so widespread among his contemporaries that many details of his life have been preserved. It will be sufficient to mention that he was born about 1410 in Nuremberg; that like a strangely large number of other famous musicians he was blind; that he traveled as far as Italy where he was greatly honored, especially by the duke of Mantua; that, late in life, he was appointed organist of the Frauenkirche at Munich; and that his tombstone is still to be found at that church.

Unfortunately, the few compositions that have come down to us under Paumann's name give only a slight idea of the significance his work must have had in the eyes of his contemporaries. His *Fundamentum organisandi* (Fundamentals of Organ Composition) of 1452 contains, in accordance with the title, mostly short instructive examples designed to illustrate the principles of composition. It also contains a few preludes (possibly not by Paumann) which, however, are much less interesting than those by Ileborgh. There remain a few actual compositions by Paumann, organ elaborations of Gregorian chants and of contemporary folk tunes, which are very beautiful indeed. One of these, entitled "Mit ganczem Willen wünsch ich Dir"— With all my heart I wish you well—is reproduced here (Fig. 16).

The last source of fifteenth-century organ music is the Buxheim

Organ Book, so called after the monastery of Buxheim near Munich where it was found sixty years ago. This is an extensive collection, probably made about 1475, and it contains, among other things, thirty preludes. These show a clear progress over those by Ileborgh, mainly

16. PAUMANN—*Mit ganczem Willen*

because of their greater extension—an evidence of the strengthened ability to carry on and develop a musical thought. The prelude which is reproduced here (Fig. 17) opens with a short passage in the free and improvisatory style of the Ileborgh preludes, continues with a section in three-voice chords, and closes in the style of the beginning.

17. BUXHEIM ORGAN BOOK—*Organ Prelude*

18. BUXHEIM ORGAN BOOK—*Facsimile*

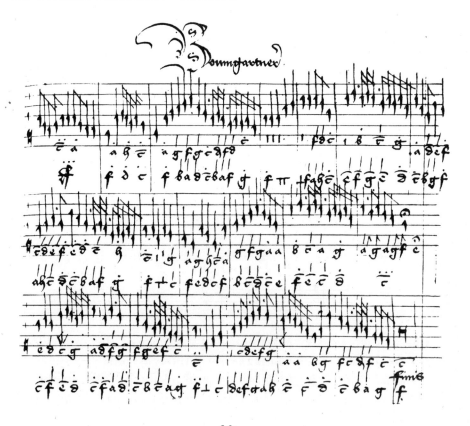

19. BAUMGARTNER—*Organ Composition*

Naturally, this composition should be played on an organ of the type which Schlick described in his book of 1511. The "sharply cutting" registers of such an instrument would give it a distinct flavor which is entirely lost in the performance on the pianoforte.

Aside from such preludes, the Buxheim Organ Book contains a great number of pieces which are organ arrangements of vocal selections. Thus compositions by the English master John Dunstable or by the Burgundian masters Dufay and Binchois, mostly secular songs written in three voice parts, occur here as organ pieces, a method which is comparable to the arrangements for pianoforte of a string quartet by Beethoven. Naturally, these arrangements are of a somewhat limited interest. Their main importance lies in the fact that they served as a model for compositions which in all probability are original organ pieces, but which nevertheless are closely modeled after the vocal style of the Burgundian school. One of these compositions, ascribed to an otherwise unknown composer, Baumgartner, is shown here in facsimile (Fig. 18) and transcription (Fig. 19).

A few stylistic details in this selection are worth pointing out. It is written in three voice parts throughout, and these frequently proceed in chordal progressions forming parallel sixth chords, such as c-e-a or d-f-b. This style was frequently used in the Burgundian School under the name of fauxbourdon, that is, false or deceptive bass, a name which in a way conforms with the modern interpretation of the sixth chord as an inversion of the triad, such as a-c-e or b-d-f. In this inversion the bass notes (a or b) of the triads are transferred, by octave transposition, into the highest voice part where they may well be said to form a "false" bass. A simple example of fauxbourdon would be that shown in Figure 20.

20.

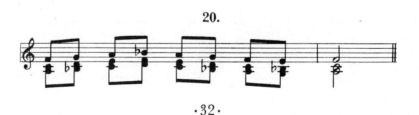

Baumgartner's composition contains this very passage, but with some remarkable modifications (Fig. 21). The difference is that the

21.

former example is entirely in the key of F, while in the latter some of the chords use the b-natural instead of the b-flat, a fact which places them into the tonality known as the Lydian mode. Various other passages in our piece, as well as in numerous others of the fifteenth century, show the use of a Lydian b-natural where the modern ear would expect a b-flat, for instance, in the fourth measure before the close.

If such passages sound wrong to the untutored listener, he may find some comfort in the fact that for many years even outstanding musical scholars have been puzzled and disturbed by these seemingly wrong notes. They have explained them in different ways—as clerical errors, as the result of an habitual negligence on the part of the composer or the copyist, or as the indication of a customary understanding among fifteenth-century musicians according to which they would play such notes as b-flats, although they are not thus marked. In conformity with such views, these scholars have provided their editions of early music with a multitude of editorial flats and sharps, changing a b-natural into a b-flat, or an f into an f-sharp, and so on. Although to the present day the problem of the accidentals in early music—or, as it is called, the problem of *musica ficta*—is not completely solved, some progress has been made in this field within the past twenty years. Generally speaking, there is now an undeniable and highly commendable tendency toward much greater moderation in the use of editorial accidentals than was customary among music historians thirty or forty years ago. It seems that two factors have been instrumental in bringing about this change. One is a greater respect for, and a truer understanding of medieval music as a great art in its own right—not, as is the current opinion, merely a "crude forerunner" of the "Golden Age" of Palestrina. This insight, which is just spreading, parallels the discovery, some fifty years ago, of medieval painting and architecture as a great art in its own right—not, as was then the current opinion, merely a barbaric presage of the "Golden Age" of Raphael and Michelangelo. The other factor is the activity of such modern composers as Schoenberg, Stravinsky, and Hindemith, who have made it abundantly clear to us that the tonal system of major and minor is no divine institution, as it was considered as late as some thirty years ago. It was a man-made conception which began to appear in the sixteenth century and became firmly entrenched after 1600, staying in power until 1900. Once this fact is recognized, the modern hearer, who more or less readily accepts the dissonances of present-day music, is well equipped to understand the musical language of the Middle Ages, a language which is different from, but no less beautiful than, that of Palestrina, Bach, or Beethoven.

1500 — THE RENAISSANCE — 1600

IN TURNING TO THE KEYBOARD MUSIC of the sixteenth century we encounter an entirely different situation from that presented by the
earlier periods. The most obvious trait of the new picture is its well-
rounded completeness, which forms a striking contrast to the frag-
mentary character of medieval keyboard music. No doubt, Johann
Gutenberg's epochal invention and its application to music [12] was a
fundamental factor in this change. Printed books, published in smaller
or larger editions, were more likely to survive the destruction of time
than single manuscript copies, and composers of renown had a much
better chance than before to have their works disseminated and preserved. While only one or two composers of keyboard music before
1500 are known to us by name, there now appears before us an uninterrupted succession of individuals forming continuous lines of
development. Moreover, while our knowledge of medieval keyboard
music is in the main restricted to one country, Germany, the advent
of the Renaissance marks the appearance of four other national
schools—in Italy, France, England, and Spain. Finally, the emergence
of a considerable number of new musical forms, such as the toccata,
the organ chorale, the ricercare, the canzona, and numerous dance
types, contributes to make the picture of Renaissance keyboard music
one of incomparably greater fullness and liveliness than that of the
preceding period.

In the middle of the fifteenth century there occurred a fundamental change of musical style, mainly under the leadership of the

masters Johannes Ockeghem (*c.* 1430–1495) and Jakob Obrecht (*c.* 1430–1505), the two earliest representatives of the Flemish School which followed after the Burgundian School of Dufay and Binchois. The most obvious traits of this change are the transition from a prevailingly secular repertory of refined and courtly chansons to a prevailingly sacred repertory of masses and motets, from three-part writing to compositions in four and five parts, from a texture consisting of a melody and two accompanying parts to a more truly polyphonic texture with equally important lines in all the parts and with an increasingly consistent use of imitation. Although these changes originally took place in the field of vocal music, they occurred once more, about half a century later, in the music for the organ. While the Burgundian style is apparent in the pieces of the Buxheim Organ Book of about 1475, Flemish influence appears clearly in the pieces of several organ composers who worked around 1500 in various parts of southern Germany and Austria. Outstanding among these is Arnolt Schlick, who was born about 1450 and died about 1520, a contemporary of the sculptor Peter Vischer and the painter Albrecht Dürer. Schlick has already been mentioned as the author of an important book on organ building which appeared in 1511. Still more important is the collection of his compositions, comprising organ pieces and a few songs with lute accompaniment, which appeared in the following year, beautifully printed by Peter Schöffer of Mainz, under the title *Tabulaturen etlicher Lobgesang und Lidlein* (Tablature of Sundry Hymns and Songs).[13] The organ pieces contained in this book are notated in essentially the same manner as all our previous examples of keyboard music—that is, with the highest part written on a staff and the lower parts indicated by letters—and it is this system of musical notation to which the term tablature refers.

What little we know about Schlick's life comes from a letter which his son wrote to him and which, with a naïve mixture of modesty and pride, he reprinted in the preface to his book. From this letter we learn that Schlick made music "on the organ, lute, harp, etc., and with the human voice for many years before emperors and kings." Indeed,

Schlick was court organist at Heidelberg, and in this position he probably had the opportunity to appear before visiting princes and rulers. It seems, however, that he did not receive the full recognition to which he was entitled, because in the same letter his son admonishes him to publish his works, saying: "Do not let thy life thus pass in silence; of what good is thy craft if nobody knows what thou canst do?"

Schlick's organ pieces all belong to the category known as *cantus-firmus* composition. This means that they are not entirely free compositions as are, for instance, the preludes or, for that matter, a sonata by Beethoven, but are contrapuntal elaborations of a preëxisting melody, the so-called *cantus firmus,* or fixed song. Most frequently this melody is taken from the large repertory of the Gregorian chant, the liturgical music of the Roman Catholic Church. In Schlick's period it was customary to present the liturgical melody, a hymn, for example, in one of the lower parts, tenor or bass, and in long equal note values, such as a whole note or even a double whole note. Around this solid foundation the other voices move in richly embellished lines of free design, so that a musical texture results in which stability and flexibility are admirably balanced. In this connection it may be mentioned that this method of composition was in use for about six hundred years, far longer than any other comparable method. It can be traced back as far as the twelfth century,[14] but its artistic possibilities were such that it was still used in the early eighteenth century by Johann Sebastian Bach, whose organ chorales include quite a number of magnificent compositions written in this manner.

Schlick's technique of *cantus-firmus* composition may be illustrated by his "Salve Regina." The *Salve Regina* is one of the four so-called "Antiphons B.M.V."—antiphons of the Blessed Virgin Mary (*Beatae Mariae Virginis*). It is one of the most famous chants of the Roman Church, and has been composed many times for voices as well as for the organ. The beginning of the liturgical melody is shown in Figure 22. In Schlick's composition this melody is given to the tenor, and here it appears as a succession of equal long notes, one to the measure (Fig. 23). Around this basic melody Schlick weaves three

22.

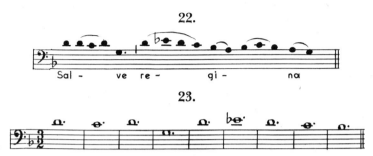

23.

contrapuntal voices, richly embroidered lines of the Flemish type which enter one after the other—somewhat in the manner of a fugue —each beginning with a boldly ascending scale.

There results a composition which is a truly great example of late

24. SCHLICK—*Salve Regina*

Gothic (or early Renaissance) art, in its balance of structural and ornamental elements as well as in its spirit of archaic austerity and solemn devoutness. It can easily be seen that pieces of this type are particularly suited for the organ since the *cantus firmus* can be played on the pedal, and thereby be sufficiently in relief to be distinguished as the structural basis of the composition. In fact, for such compositions the pianoforte is a rather unsatisfactory medium, and even the modern organ usually fails to bring about that particular liveliness and variety of sound which resulted naturally from the "sharply cutting" stops of Schlick's organ. Nevertheless, the great artistic qualities of Schlick's "Salve Regina" (Fig. 24) are always apparent regardless of the medium of performance.

Most of the organ pieces contained in Schlick's *Tabulaturen* are of the same type, employing a liturgical *cantus firmus* in long notes in one of the lower voice parts. One composition, however, is remarkably different, for here the borrowed melody is in the soprano and is presented, not as a rigid structure of sustained tones, but as a flowing melody of great tenderness and beauty. This composition is called "Maria zart"—O sweet Mary—(Fig. 25), and it is no accident that

25. SCHLICK—*Maria zart*

this is the only one of Schlick's organ compositions which is based, not on a Gregorian chant (which, naturally, would have a Latin title) , but on a hymn in the German vernacular. The melody of this hymn is of a quite different nature from that of plainsong. It is more tuneful and folk-like, more regular and symmetrical, and its clearly separated phrases foreshadow the Lutheran chorale which came to the fore some twenty years after Schlick. It is an example—one of the earliest known —of a new body of religious music, expressing not the exalted thought of the Church but the pious devotion of the people—of a musical tradition growing up, as it were, not inside the church walls but in the sunlight of the surrounding yard. Schlick fully grasped the particular significance of this melody and treated it accordingly. Instead of using it as a purely structural foundation he places it in the full light of the soprano voice, freely exhibiting its natural charm, embellishing it by subtle ornamentations, and enhancing it by two contrapuntal voices which are remarkable for the exquisite clarity of their lines. Another interesting trait of these contrapuntal parts is the skillful incorporation of thematic material taken over from the main melody, according to the principles of imitation. Thus, the middle voice part enters in measure 5 with a (free) imitation of the preceding four measures of the soprano. Imitation at a close distance is found in measures 1 to 3 of system VII (soprano and tenor) and in measures 1 to 3 of system IX (soprano and bass). Yet another realization of the principle of imitation is exemplified by measures 10 to 11 from the beginning, and measures 1 to 2 of system V. Here the lower part, instead of following the melody in imitation, anticipates it, a method which is known as Vorimitation,[15] and which plays an important part in the chorale preludes by Bach.

While the Gothic music of Germany reached a late culmination in compositions like those of Schlick, musicians of other countries were following novel trends which indicated more clearly the influence of Renaissance mentality. It is not easy to state in a general way the difference between the musical Gothic and the musical Renaissance, nor to indicate the line of demarcation between these two periods. The most obvious mark of distinction, that of the shift of emphasis from the sacred to the secular field, is not valid in a general sense for, although secular forms such as the madrigal did accompany the rise of Renaissance music, the sacred forms, motets and masses, continued to play a dominant role throughout the sixteenth century. In the particular province of keyboard music, however, the change is more clearly marked than in vocal music, owing to the rise to prominence of a repertory of distinctly secular affiliation: dance music. Examples of dance music are not entirely lacking in the fourteenth and fifteenth centuries. Their scarcity, however, together with evidence gained from literary sources, points to the fact that the development of dancing and of dance music was severely handicapped by the opposition of the Church. One may be doubtful as to whether the clergy was ever completely successful in its efforts to suppress dancing, but it seems that its influence was strong enough to prevent dance music from rising above the level of mere utility music into the sphere of musical art.

This situation changed suddenly and completely with the advent of the sixteenth century. The spiritual emancipation of the Renaissance led to a real outburst of dancing, and mankind reacted against the long suppression of a natural instinct. Indeed, if there is any period in the history of music which could justly be called the century of the dance, it is the sixteenth century. At no other time, perhaps with the exception of the present day, was dancing so universally practiced. Side by side, we find ceremonial court dances, dignified dances of the burghers, and frolicsome peasant dances. We find the most exquisite manners, and the most disorderly conduct. One report tells us about joyful round dances under the linden tree, another describes affected steps and courteous bows in gilded ballrooms, while a third decries indecent cavortings in the tavern. Dance fashion changed fast, and shifted from country to country. In the late fifteenth and early sixteenth centuries the ceremonial dance of the French-Burgundian court, the *basse danse,* was prominent. About 1520 this was replaced by the Spanish court dance, the *pavane,* while, about 1550, the Italians took the lead with the *passamezzo.* Side by side with these three main dances were numerous others—the French *branle,* the Italian *saltarello,* the German *Hoftanz.* During the second half of the century appeared those types which were destined to form the basis of the seventeenth- and eighteenth-century suite: the German *allemande,* the French *courante,* the Spanish *sarabande,* and the English *gigue.*

All the dances of the Renaissance are characterized by a certain sturdiness and robustness which makes them appear more "earthbound" than the refined and graceful dances of the seventeenth century. As an example, I have reproduced a "Spanyöler Tancz" (Fig. 26) from a German manuscript of about 1520.[16]

The title of this dance does not refer to a Spanish origin, but to a popular melody of the fifteenth century, "Il re di Spagna" (The King of Spain), which is incorporated into our composition, its melody being an elaborately ornamented variation of the original tune. Weck's dance is an example of the French basse danse, which was also cultivated in Italy during the fifteenth century. It shows the characteristic trochaic rhythm (a long note followed by a short) in slow triple meter which is usually found in the basse danses.

26. WECK—*Spanyöler Tancz*

The pavane originated in Spain, where it formed an integral part of the court ceremonies under the Emperors Charles V and Philip II. Its name is probably derived from the Latin word *pavo,* that is, peacock. The pavane was a very stately dance, usually in slow duple meter, executed with many intricate steps which may well have been suggested by the strutting and stalking of the exotic bird. From Spain it spread to France as well as to that country which was soon to become the great antagonist of Spain, England. An interesting description of this dance was given by a French nobleman attending a feast at the court of Henry VIII. He says: "At this festival the king took in his sister. I saw them often dancing the Spanish pavane which is so perfectly fit for showing charm combined with highness. I could never get enough of this picture since the passages were so matchlessly danced, the steps so perfectly executed, the standing still so expressly marked that one had to confess never having seen anything similar. I too share this opinion, though I saw the queens of Spain and Scotland dancing this dance well."

Easily the most popular of all pavane tunes was the one [17] reproduced in Figure 27. This tune is particularly interesting because one

27. SIXTEENTH CENTURY PAVANE

of the greatest keyboard composers of the sixteenth century, the Spaniard Antonio de Cabezón (1510–1566), used it as a theme for variations, under the title "Diferencias sobra la Pavana Italiana" (Variations on the Italian Pavane). Actually, the theme of Cabezón's

28.

29. CABEZÓN—*Diferencias sobra la Pavana Italiana*

variations agrees with the above tune only in its first half, the continuation representing a different version. As is usually the case in the variations of the sixteenth and seventeenth centuries, this example starts immediately with the first variation, without a previous statement of the theme in its simplest form. The obvious reason for this procedure is that these melodies were universally known at the time. It may also be noticed that Cabezón's five variations run on continuously, each one being connected with the next by a short transitional passage. This composition affords another example of that mixed tonality, partly F-major and partly Lydian, which was discussed in the preceding chapter in connection with Baumgartner's piece from the Buxheim Organ Book. In the first measures of this example we find formations which, from the modern point of view, would have to be harmonized in F-major, in other words, with a b-flat throughout (Fig. 28). Cabezón, however, writes them in the Lydian mode, with a b-natural (Fig. 29).

In addition to variations Cabezón wrote a great number of liturgical organ pieces, similar in character to Schlick's "Salve Regina." Particularly remarkable among these are his *versos*—short organ pieces which were used in connection with the singing of the psalms. The psalms, as is well known, consist of a number of verses which are sung in the Roman service to one of the eight psalm tones, that is, short recitation formulae, one for each of the eight church modes. Figure 30 shows the *Sextus tonus* (Sixth psalm tone) with some of

30. PSALM—*Dixit Dominus*

the verses of Psalm 109, "Dixit Dominus" (Psalm 110 of the King James Bible, "The Lord said unto the Lord").

In the sixteenth and seventeenth centuries the monotony resulting from the numerous repetitions of the same short melodic formula was relieved by the use of the organ, which supplanted the even-numbered verses by short organ pieces, usually contrapuntal elaborations of the plainsong melody which now appears as a *cantus firmus*. Cabezón was one of the first to write such pieces which, owing to their

31. CABEZÓN—*Versos del sexto tono*

liturgical origin and position, were called *versos, versets, Versetten,* and so on. His four "Versos del sexto tono" are reproduced in Figure 31.

In the first verset the plainsong melody (*canto llano*) appears in the soprano (*tiple*), and subsequently in the alto, tenor, and bass. It will be seen that in all the versets the first three notes of the Gregorian psalm tone are omitted. This omission is explained by the fact that according to the Gregorian tradition the initial notes (the so-called *initium*) are used only for the first psalm verses, while the other verses start with the so-called monotone (or tenor) that follows after the initium. The style of Cabezón's versets is clearly imitative. In the versets numbers 2, 3, and 4 the imitation is based on two subjects, one for the first half, the other for the second.

No serious-minded student can fail to recognize the outstanding artistic quality of these little pieces. Within a handful of measures there arises a complete work of art, full of life and all the more animated, in a deeper sense, as it renounces all external signs of animation. Far removed from any implication of "Spanish temperament" as current thought understands or misunderstands it, this music is austere and reserved, a product of the same spirit which reveals itself in the works of Arnolt Schlick and Johann Sebastian Bach. Not improperly, Cabezón has been called "the Spanish Bach." In fact, there are not many composers before Bach—and not one after him—who by reason of profundity of thought, seriousness of purpose, and, last but not least, contrapuntal mastery, more properly belong in his company.

The Italian organ music of the sixteenth century found an early representative of outstanding significance in Girolamo Cavazzoni who, in 1542 and 1543, published two collections of organ pieces under the title *Intavolatura cioè recercari canzoni himni magnificati* (Tablature,[18] that is to say, Ricercars, Canzonas, Hymns, Magnificats). In the preface of the first book (which he dedicated to the famous Cardinal Bembo) Cavazzoni designates its contents as *primitie della mia giovinezza* (first fruit of my youth) and refers to himself as *anchor quasi fanciullo* (still almost a boy). He therefore can hardly have been

32. CAVAZZONI—*Kyrie*

more than twenty years old when he wrote these pieces, and if this assumption is correct, he is one of the most astonishing child prodigies to be found in music history. Indeed, his compositions show a maturity such as may well be expected at the close, rather than the beginning, of a life devoted to musical composition. His second book contains several organ masses, in other words, organ compositions based on the text and the plainsong melodies of the mass.

Shown in Figure 32 is the first Kyrie of his "Missa Apostolorum." Like Schlick's "Salve Regina" and "Maria zart," this is a *cantus-firmus* composition, and it is based on the plainsong melody of the first Kyrie from the Gregorian Mass IV (Fig. 33). The treatment of this melody

33. GREGORIAN MASS NO. IV—*First Kyrie*

is somewhat similar to that in Schlick's "Maria zart," but goes a good deal farther in the direction of subtlety and expression. In both compositions the *cantus firmus* is used in the soprano, and the contrapuntal voice parts occasionally take up snatches of it. While Schlick, however, uses his melody nearly in its original form, aside from ornamenting figurations, Cavazzoni changes the plainsong into something entirely different and new, by freely modifying its rhythmic structure and by expanding its contents through the addition of expressive melodic material.

A contemporary of Cavazzoni was Andrea Gabrieli (1510?–1586), organist of St. Mark's at Venice. He and his nephew Giovanni Gabrieli (1557–1612) are usually spoken of together as the "two Gabrielis"— a somewhat misleading designation because Giovanni, being almost fifty years the junior of Andrea, represents an altogether different period of music. Andrea Gabrieli's importance in the field of keyboard music lies mainly in the establishment of a new organ style which is free from contrapuntal elements and in which idiomatic keyboard formations such as full chords and scale passages predominate. To be sure, these elements were not entirely new. They had been used in the early preludes, and Andrea Gabrieli used them for compositions of a similar character. However, in his hands these elements became much more integrated and are amalgamated into a homogeneous composition consisting of broad, massive chords intertwined with impressively rising or falling scale passages. One of his Intonazioni (intonation, that is, prelude) serves to illustrate this style (Fig. 34).

34. A. GABRIELI—*Intonazione*

Despite its shortness, this composition fully conveys the impression of festive pomp which is a characteristic trait of the Venetian School. One cannot help seeing in this music a reflection of the wealth and splendor of Venice, with its magnificent cathedral of St. Mark's, the most celebrated church of Christendom before the erection of St. Peter's at Rome. St. Mark's was the first church to have two organs, and the positions of first and second organist of St. Mark's were the most highly regarded and most highly rewarded of the time. In 1566 Andrea Gabrieli became second organist of St. Mark's, succeeding a younger man who at the same time was promoted to the position of the first organist; this man was Claudio Merulo (1533–1604). The fact that Merulo, at the age of thirty-three years, was appointed to the highest position an organist of the sixteenth century could attain, is sufficient evidence of his excellence as an organ player. His excellence as an organ composer appears just as clearly in his numerous compositions for this instrument, particularly in his toccatas.

Of all the forms of keyboard music, the toccata is the most strictly idiomatic, similar in this respect to the prelude from which, in all probability, it originated. The very name toccata, derived from the Italian word *toccare* (to touch or to strike), indicates a close relationship to the keyboard technique, and, in fact, throughout its development, from the sixteenth century to the present day, the toccata has always and exclusively remained a type of keyboard music. The earliest toccatas, composed around 1550 by Andrea Gabrieli and some of his contemporaries, are written throughout in the same style of scale-entwined chords which he used in his intonazioni. Being considerably more extended, however, they do not escape the danger of monotony inherent in so limited an idiom. Merulo showed the great possibilities of the toccata by amplifying its formal structure and enlarging its stylistic resources. His toccatas usually consist of three or five sections written alternately in a free, improvisatory style derived from the early toccatas, and in the strictly contrapuntal style of the contemporary ricercar.[19] It is interesting to notice that the toccata form consisting of five sections was taken over, in the seventeenth century, by the North-German organ masters, notably Buxtehude, and that from there it found its way into the toccatas of Bach. Merulo's toccatas are no less remarkable for their structural principles than for their stylistic traits, particularly in the free sections. In these sections we find much the same elements—full chords and keyboard passages —which form the basis of the early toccatas, but they are used with incomparably greater skill and imagination. The passages show much more varied contours and a more interesting design which frequently adopts an expressive meaning. In the harmonic field, the scope of the chords is considerably broadened and the structural significance of the harmonies is clearly brought out by well-prepared cadences and modulations. Finally, the musical texture no longer consists of chords and passages only, but includes contrapuntal elements. The chordal blocks of the early toccata are replaced by a more continuous style of writing involving voice progressions which lead from one chord to the next. All these traits combine to make Merulo's toccatas highly impressive works of musical art, magnificent structures of sonorous pillars, surfaces, and lines (Fig. 35). More than any other type of keyboard music they represent a reflection of the resplendent grandeur of the late Renaissance period.

We shall now turn to another country which made important contributions to the keyboard music of the Renaissance: England. The English music of the late sixteenth century, that is, of the Elizabethan period, is rather well known to musicians and musical amateurs, partly through its magnificent repertory of secular songs, the madrigals, and partly through its keyboard music, known as "virginalistic music." Unfortunately, the splendor, musical as well as literary, of this period has put the preceding development into a somewhat undeserved eclipse. Not until recently did the early Tudor composers such as Tallis and Taverner find the recognition due to them. While these masters wrote only vocal music for the church there were others who provided organ music. Outstanding among these is John Redford (1485–1545), who was organist of St. Paul's Cathedral in the reign of Henry VIII. Redford's compositions are all liturgical organ pieces, and a number of them are impressive examples of genuine church style.[20]

On the whole, however, English keyboard composers of the sixteenth century were more successful with the harpsichord than with
the organ, and in dances or variations more than in liturgical pieces or
contrapuntal compositions. The earliest source of English harpsichord
music, a manuscript in the British Museum dating from about 1525,
contains a number of interesting dance pieces, among which a "Hornepype" by Hugh Aston (*c.* 1480–1522?) is easily the most outstanding.
In fact, it is no exaggeration to say that this is one of the most extraordinary pieces in the entire literature of keyboard music. Its
singularity rests on a combination of three features: an extremely
simple scheme of harmonies; a rich flow of melodies; and a dynamic
structure rising to ever higher levels of intensity and liveliness.

35. MERULO—*Toccata*

Harmonically the entire piece, from the first to the last of its 118 measures, consists of nothing but an alternation of dominant and tonic, of a c-major chord and an f-major chord, each chord serving as the harmonic basis for one measure (Fig. 36).

36.

In a striking contrast to this utterly simple scheme of harmonies is the abundant flow of melodies above it, melodies so full of variety and imagination that they completely obscure, from the listener's point of view, the harmonic primitiveness. As a matter of fact, I remember having played this composition for many years without ever noticing its harmonic scheme, because my attention was so exclusively absorbed by its other, more highly developed, qualities.

The third feature, that of formal structure, is perhaps the most remarkable of all, considering the period in which the "Hornepype" was written. Its mere length, 118 measures, is quite exceptional in sixteenth-century instrumental music. The really astonishing fact, however, is that this length is the result, not of continuation on the same level (as is the rule in most sixteenth-century music), but of an organic growth and development which is rarely encountered in music before the sonatas and symphonies of the Viennese Classics. It is quite possible that our composition reflects the actual dancing of a hornpipe, though in an idealized style. If this is true, then the hornpipe, as danced around 1500, must have been a most extraordinary presentation, running the whole gamut of emotions from idyllic contemplation to violent excitement. Aston's "Hornepype" begins with eleven measures in the character of a slow introduction, based upon gentle and idyllic motives. Then there appears a real dance motive with a strong rhythmic pulse, opening a short section which may be inscribed allegro molto moderato.[21] This, in turn, is followed by a third section, un poco più mosso, in which fast motives prevail and which finally brings us to the last and most extended section, allegro, which is a truly pyrotechnical display of lively motives and captivating rhythms. A breath-taking pace is maintained throughout this section, and it is not until the final eight measures that a slower motion takes place, suggesting a relaxation from the intoxication of the dance (Fig. 37).

Skipping over half a century, we now turn to the keyboard music of the Elizabethan period, usually designated as "virginalistic music," after the virginal, the English sixteenth-century type of harpsichord. This is an extremely important period of early keyboard music and one which deserves much fuller consideration than can be given here. Its most obvious contribution is the development and establishment of an idiomatic piano—properly speaking, harpsichord—style, as distinguished from a style designed primarily for the organ or derived from vocal models. Numerous elements of the pianistic technique—rapid scales, broken-chord figures, quick passages in parallel thirds and sixths, broken octaves, and so on—appear here and are exploited with an astonishing degree of virtuosity. As may well be expected, the compositions in which this virtuosity is carried to the highest point are not necessarily those of the highest artistic significance. By and large, however, the virginalistic repertory shows a happy balance between technical and artistic achievement.

The most important source of virginalistic literature is the Fitzwilliam Virginal Book,[22] a manuscript collection of nearly three hundred pieces, brought together during the first and second decades of the seventeenth century. Among the numerous composers represented in this and other books, three may be singled out as outstanding representatives of three successive generations: William Byrd, who was born about 1543; John Bull, born about 1563; and Orlando Gibbons, born in 1583, nearly one hundred years before Bach. Although Byrd seems to have been the first to cultivate the harpsichord extensively, he reached an artistic high-point which dwarfs all the other virginalists, except Gibbons. In a way, the development leading from the

37. ASTON—*Hornepype*

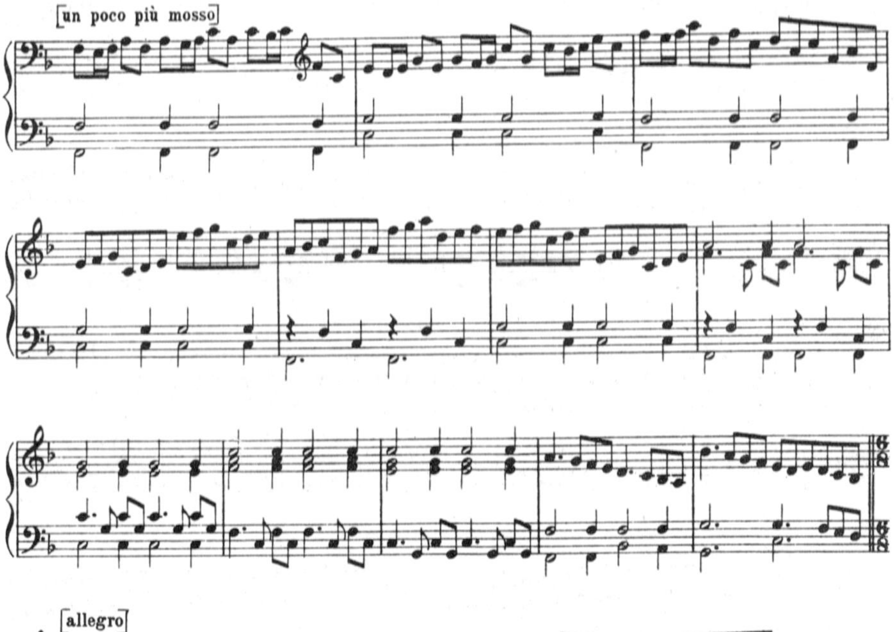
[un poco più mosso]
[allegro]

·64·

former to the latter may be compared to that leading from the early Haydn and Mozart to the late Beethoven. Indeed the keyboard works of Byrd are just as great in their simplicity and natural charm as are those by Gibbons in their consummate mastery and utmost refinement. John Bull was famous mainly as a touring virtuoso, just as famous in his day as was Franz Liszt in the nineteenth century. Many of his pieces exhibit a truly stupendous display of virtuosity, hardly second in difficulty to that of Liszt's compositions. While in these pieces exhibitionism takes much the better part of artistic achievement, Bull also wrote a number of compositions which are remarkable for their high musical quality.

Among the various forms cultivated by the Elizabethan keyboard composers two are of particular interest: variations and dances. We encountered a first example of variations in those by the Spaniard Cabezón. All evidence points to Spain as the native country of this form, a form which, by the way, is the oldest of all musical forms still in existence. When the variation form was transplanted into England it underwent a most significant change of style and expression. While the Spanish variations are serious and introspective, full of inner tension and restraint, those of the virginalists are gay and carefree, light-hearted and sparkling. Cabezón's variations on "La Pavana Italiana" and Byrd's variations on an English folk tune, "The Carman's Whistle," stand in about the same relationship as a composition by Bach to one by Mozart. Figure 38 reproduces the first four of Byrd's eight variations.

The dance music of the virginalists is of particular importance, for it represents the culmination of a form which, as we have seen, was extensively cultivated in many countries throughout the sixteenth century. The artistic superiority of their dances to those of any other country is indeed most striking. With composers like Byrd, Bull, and Gibbons dance music passed, as it were, from the hands of respectable craftsmen into the hands of creative artists. Their dances form the final link in a process of idealization similar to the one which led, more than one hundred years later, to the allemandes, courantes, and

38. BYRD—*The Carman's Whistle*

VAR. I.

sarabandes in the suites of Bach. Unlike Bach, however, who used all the dance types which had been developed before him, the English masters concentrated their artistic efforts mainly on one single dance, the pavane, usually combining it with a second dance in triple meter and faster speed, the galliard. It will be remembered that the pavane is the oldest of all the numerous dance types which evolved in the sixteenth century. The striking preference for this dance may be interpreted as an example of English traditionalism and conservatism. But traditionalism in itself is certainly not sufficient to bring about artistic results, a truism which, by the way, is nowhere better illustrated than in the history of English music in general. In the present case, however, the pertinacity with which the English musicians clung to the pavane enabled them to raise this dance type to an artistic significance incomparably higher than was the case in other countries where change of fashion was the foremost consideration.

A short composition by William Byrd, called "Pavane, The Earle of Salisbury," serves as an illustration of this form (Fig. 39). But the

39. BYRD—*Pavane, The Earle of Salisbury*

fullest development of the English pavane is reached in the compositions by Orlando Gibbons. Gibbons is a typical example of a "late" master whose *fin-de-siècle* personality exudes the fascination of an approaching decadence, but whose creative power is still unbroken— he was not dissimilar in this respect to his contemporary Shakespeare. His pavane entitled "The Lord of Salisbury His Pavin" (Fig. 40) is a masterpiece whose utter refinement and spirituality recall the late sonatas of Beethoven. Like many pavanes of the sixteenth century, it consists of three sections each of which develops a different thought. Particularly noteworthy is Gibbons' mastery of the musical phrase. This he treats, not, as is so frequently the case, in the stereotyped pattern of a four-measure unit, but as an extended and continuous flow of energy which carries the musical thought far beyond its expected limit.

It is interesting to compare the English dance music of the Elizabethan period with the dances written at the same time in Germany. Far removed from the artistic elaboration of the English masters, the German composers of the late sixteenth century were content with writing simple dance tunes of a folk-like character, such as were used for dancing among the peasants, burghers, and noblemen. A great number of these dances have been preserved in the books of Nikolaus Ammerbach (1571), Bernhard Schmid (1577), and Augustus Nörmiger (1598), and they present a very charming picture of German folk life at the close of the Renaissance. There are dances which are built upon folk songs, for example (in translation), "We All Like a Good Drink" or "Love in the Month of May"; there are court dances for the festivities of the nobility, for instance, a "First Mask of the Widow of the Elector of Saxony"; there are character dances such as "The Moors' Pageant," "The Shepherd's Dance," "The Dance of Death," or "The Procession of the Three Holy Kings," which were probably danced in characteristic costumes. Finally there are dances like "Ballo Anglese" (English Dance), "Ballo Milanese" (Milanese Dance), "A Good Polish Dance," and "Ungaresca" (Hungarian Dance), which are indicative of the cosmopolitan character of dance

40. GIBBONS—*The Lord of Salisbury His Pavin*

·71·

music towards the end of the sixteenth century. Two selections from
the book of August Nörmiger are given here as an illustration: first

41. NÖRMIGER—*Der Mohren Auftzugkh*

(Fig. 41), "Der Mohren Auttzugkh" (The Moors' Pageant); then
(Fig. 42), "Der Schefer Tantz" (The Shepherd's Dance)—which
also includes "Der Sprung darauff" (The Jumping Dance thereafter),
and "Der Kerabe" (modern German *Kehraus*, i.e., sweep out), the
German equivalent to what we call "Good night, Ladies."

The last composer to be considered in this chapter is the Dutchman
Jan Pieterzoon Sweelinck, a master who, although firmly rooted in
the tradition of the Renaissance, casts his shadow far ahead into the
period of Baroque music. A contemporary and a close friend of John
Bull, he was as famous for his organ playing as was the English master
for his virtuosity on the harpsichord. The organ concerts which Sweelinck gave regularly through many years in a church at Amsterdam
were an international sensation and attracted admirers and pupils

42. NÖRMIGER—*Der Schefer Tantz*

Der Sprung Darauff

Der Kerabe

43. SWEELINCK—*Mein junges Leben hat ein End*

from all over Europe. The majority of his pupils came from Germany, which at that time was just emerging as an important member in the family of musical nations, and he well deserved the name given him: *deutscher Organistenmacher* (maker of German organists). He absorbed the figural harpsichord style and the variation technique of the virginalists, combined them with contrapuntal elements derived from Italian models, and passed these achievements on to men like Samuel Scheidt, Heinrich Scheidemann, Melchior Schildt, and Jakob Praetorius, who stand at the outset of the development leading, one hundred years later, to Johann Sebastian Bach. Most of Sweelinck's keyboard works are extended, sometimes over-extended, organ compositions in which the resources of the instrument as well as the potentialities of imitative counterpoint are exploited with a high degree of technical skill and of what might be called "learned imagination."

More sympathetic to the modern mind are his variations, some of which are outstanding for their display of truly musical ingenuity. His variations on "Mein junges Leben hat ein End" (My young life comes to its end) figure among the dozen of the greatest masterworks in this genre, hardly second to Bach's *Goldberg Variations,* Beethoven's *Diabelli Variations,* or Brahms's *Variations on a Theme by Handel.* Although these variations are usually classified as harpsichord pieces, they find their most impressive realization if played on a Baroque organ with its unlimited variety of tonal effects. The first two and the last of Sweelinck's variations are reproduced in Figure 43.

1600 — THE EARLY BAROQUE PERIOD — 1675

WITH THIS CHAPTER we enter a new period of music history, namely the period of Baroque music which extends from approximately 1600 to 1750. Before turning to a consideration of the keyboard music of this period it may not be amiss to say a few words about the general connotation and ramifications of the term Baroque. This term, which probably comes from a Portuguese word *barrocco* (that is, a pearl of irregular shape), is frequently used in a decidedly depreciatory sense. Webster explains it as meaning "grotesque," or "in corrupt taste." Its application to the fine arts, in which it has been used for a long time, was originally based on the idea that seventeenth-century style in architecture and painting was a debased Renaissance style. This opinion, however, was thoroughly revised about 1900 by Heinrich Wölfflin who was the first to point out the positive achievements and great artistic qualities of Baroque art, and who exonerated the term Baroque from any implication of inferiority. Unfortunately, musicians to the present day have been reluctant to adopt this view. Clinging to the orthodox interpretation of the word, they naturally resent calling a period "in corrupt taste" which culminates in one of the greatest figures of all music history, Johann Sebastian Bach. However, through its use in the fine arts the term has actually lost its derogatory meaning, and has become established as a noncommittal designation for an important period of cultural development. Its adoption in music is to be advocated mainly on the ground that it places a well-defined period of music history within its proper frame. Naturally, in speaking of Baroque music one has to abandon completely any

·77·

meaning of "grotesque" or "in corrupt taste." The latter designation may possibly be applied to certain late Baroque styles leading to the next period, the Rococo, which indeed shows signs of corruption and poor taste. Baroque music proper, however, perhaps more than any other period of music history, is a period of "good taste." It shows a truly exemplary balance of form and contents, of purpose and means. It shows a mixture of dignity and charm, of expressiveness and restraint, which could be achieved, perhaps, only in those days when men felt just as free to enjoy their earthly lives as they felt themselves bound to the laws of God and the Church.

As mentioned previously, the period of Baroque music extends from about 1600 to 1750. Both these dates are about fifty years later than those usually given for the Baroque period in the fine arts. This, however, is no objection against the ideological association of both periods. It is only one of several examples illustrating the fact that processes of cultural innovation or modification find an earlier reflection in the fine arts than in music which, by its very nature, is the latest of all the arts. At any rate, the dates 1600 and 1750 are well-defined and highly important landmarks in music history. The first date marks the establishment of a new musical style, known as monody—in other words, accompanied solo song—which breaks the sixteenth-century tradition of polyphonic choral music. Thus, motets, masses, and madrigals gave way to arias, cantatas, and operas. The date 1750, on the other hand, is the year of death of the man who represents the epitome and summit of Baroque music, Johann Sebastian Bach.

The keyboard music of the Baroque period is extremely rich and diversified. Three nations stand in the foreground: Italy, Germany, and France, with England being a "good runner-up." Although each of these countries made its specific contributions, there was a considerable exchange of ideas and much coöperation on an international basis, in fact more than in any other period of music history. This situation makes the picture extremely interesting but, for that matter, much more difficult to trace than in the Renaissance or in the nineteenth century. The mere number of important composers in this period far exceeds that in any other period of comparable extent. If the one and one-half centuries from 1790 to 1940 can be characterized by, say, twenty really important names, there are at least double that number of important masters from 1600 to 1750. Under these circumstances our consideration of Baroque keyboard music must of necessity be a sketchy one, restricted to a somewhat arbitrary selection of composers and works. In the present chapter we shall consider the first half of the Baroque period from 1600 to 1675.

At the beginning of Baroque keyboard music stands one of the most fascinating personalities of music history: the Italian Girolamo Frescobaldi, organist of St. Peter's in Rome, who lived from 1583 to 1643. Although his name is rather widely known, his compositions have, to the present day, remained in the obscurity of scholarly editions. A somewhat tragicomic illustration of this situation is given by the fact that the only pieces which, under the title "Fugues by Frescobaldi," have found their way into some collections of early music and, hence, into the hands of music students, are definitely spurious. Their style is that of a period even later than Bach, and it is possible that some such composer as Clementi wrote them in what he believed to be Frescobaldi's style. Genuine compositions by Frescobaldi are, one must confess, difficult to understand and appreciate. His musical personality is a unique mixture of an imaginative artist and a reflective scholar, a combination which is all but incomprehensible to the modern mind, but which is by no means out of place in a century which produced such universal minds as Descartes, Leibnitz, and Mersenne. Frescobaldi's tonal language is full of unusual formations and peculiar idioms such as are not found with other composers of his day. Queer as these peculiarities appear at first glance, they reveal, upon closer study, that quality of inner logic and veracity which bespeaks the true creative genius. True enough, his music entirely lacks the "immediate appeal" which the modern hearer expects and demands. But to the listener who is willing to pay the price of patient study it offers the recompense of never becoming tiring, of always revealing new points of interest and new features of significance. The reproduced examples (Fig. 44), chosen from different compositions by Frescobaldi, serve to illustrate the bold individuality of his style, a style which frequently assaults the ear, but always satisfies the mind.

44.

Frescobaldi's keyboard compositions are chiefly of three types: toccatas, variations, and fugal pieces. His toccatas naturally invite a comparison with those written by Merulo some twenty years before. Although this was a relatively short span of time it was sufficient to bring about a drastic change. If Merulo's toccatas, written in a broad and pompous fresco style, represent the grandiose splendor of the late Renaissance, those by Frescobaldi reflect the nervous excitement, the frenzied restlessness of the early Baroque period. The great architectural masses and broad surfaces of the Merulo toccata have disappeared, superseded by a disintegrated structure of numerous small segments, by a multiplicity of formations which seems to recognize no other law than that of variety, change, and surprise. Instead of long-held triads moving slowly in a restricted modal realm, Frescobaldi offers bold and willful harmony with abrupt changes of tonality; instead of extended linear contours we find restless and short, jerky motives; and the evenly measured flow of motion is replaced by a nervous and pressing rhythm, full of syncopations and complicated cross-rhythms. Shown here is a toccata in F-major (Fig. 45).

Only a great genius can work in such an idiom without being caught in its pitfalls. A demonstration of this fact may hardly be necessary, but it actually exists in the toccatas of one of Frescobaldi's pupils, Michelangelo Rossi (fl. 1625–1650); Rossi's toccatas are interesting because they show Frescobaldi's style changed from spontaneous imagination to formalistic mannerism. Incidentally, Michelangelo Rossi shares the fate of his illustrious teacher in being known chiefly through a spurious composition: an "Andantino and Allegro" by "Abbate Michel Angelo Rossi (1620–1660)" which has found its way into nearly all the current collections of early keyboard music, sometimes in a prominent position as the opening piece.[23] Actually this composition is a typical example of eighteenth-century Rococo style, and was probably composed by one Abbate Lorenzo de Rossi who lived from 1720 to 1794. Today it is difficult to understand why a piece like this could ever have been ascribed to a composer of the early seventeenth century (imagine a painting by Gainsborough be-

·83·

ing ascribed to Rembrandt!) , but the fact that even so outstanding a scholar as Hugo Riemann let himself be deceived (although he was suspicious) shows to what an extent the very rudiments of musical style criticism were unknown forty or fifty years ago.

Passing over the variations by Frescobaldi, his compositions in fugal style deserve some explanatory remarks. As has been pointed out, the compositions going under the title "Fugues by Frescobaldi" are spurious. As a matter of fact, the fugue, as we know it from Bach, did not develop until the last quarter of the seventeenth century, several decades after Frescobaldi's death. Prior to this time there existed various other types of a related character, such as the ricercar, the canzona, the fantasia, and the capriccio. All these, as well as the fugue, belong to the general category of instrumental compositions in imitative counterpoint. This means that they are written in a fixed number, usually three or four, of individual voice parts, and that a characteristic "subject" or "theme" which is stated as the beginning in one voice alone, is successively imitated by the others and recurs throughout the entire composition in the various voice parts. The subsequent schematic graph, in which each voice of a four-part fugue (or ricercar, and so on) is represented by a horizontal line, may be helpful in clarifying the principle of imitative counterpoint. The letter S indicates the subject of the fugue, while the dotted lines between successive statements of the subject indicate free, or non-thematic, counterpoint.

```
        S................................S.........................................................................
S.......................................................................S....................S..............
            S...........................................S......................................................
        S...........................................................S..........................................
```

Aside from stylistic differences conditioned by their earlier date, the pre-fugal forms, ricercar, canzona, and so on, differ from the fugue proper mainly in their formal structure. The fugue is normally mono-thematic, that is, it is based on one theme only. The earlier types, on the other hand, are usually polythematic; they fall into several sections each of which has its own subject. Another structural trait of the fugue, and one of even greater significance, is the systematic use of episodes, passages which do not contain the subject and which thus serve as a relief from the tension created by the appearance of the subject. In the older types of imitative counterpoint the tendency is to use the subject continuously, without the balancing effect of episodes.

Of particular interest is the history of the canzona. This developed, in the first half of the sixteenth century, from the French chanson of the period, a type of vocal music in the general style of sixteenth-century imitative counterpoint, but distinguished from the contemporary motet by more lively themes, more pungent rhythms, and more clearly marked phrases and sections; not to mention the fact that the texts were amorous, frequently with a good sprinkling of lascivious allusions. Considering these features, particularly the last, it is not surprising that these chansons acquired an immense popularity, but in fairness to Renaissance mentality it must be said that they became even more successful in a textless variety, that is, in the form of pieces similar in style and structure to the vocal forms, but written for instrumental ensembles or for a keyboard instrument. Such pieces were written mainly by Italian composers and therefore became known under the Italian designation *canzona francese* (French chanson) or, simply, canzona. It is interesting to notice that through its instrumental variety the frivolous chanson became the ancestor of the most important form of modern music, the sonata, the original name of which was *canzona da sonare*—canzona for sounding on instruments. This development, however, is not our concern since it took place in the field of violin music. The keyboard canzona developed in a different direction, leading to the fugue. How it was possible for one and the same form to develop into two so entirely different things as the sonata and the fugue is perhaps somewhat puzzling at first thought. The answer lies in the fact that the violin composers emphasized the sectional structure of the canzona, gradually enlarging the sections and separating them into a number of distinct movements in contrasting character and tempo. The keyboard composers, on the other hand, emphasized the stylistic traits of the canzona: the contrapuntal texture and the use of imitation. In the latter field, moreover, the development took the direction toward unification rather than toward separation. Frescobaldi took a first and important step in this direction by creating a new type of keyboard canzona, known as variation canzona. This means that the various fugal sections of the canzona are based, not on different themes—as had been the case—but on rhythmic variants of one and the same theme. For example, one of his canzonas falls into three fugal sections with the subjects shown in Figure 46. Each of the three sections closes with a

46.

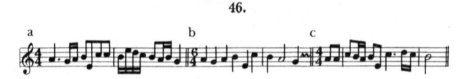

short cadenza in the free style of the toccata and marked *Adasio* in the original. Thus the musical motion and energy in each section presents a picture similar to the damming up of a flowing river—a type of motion which is extremely characteristic of Frescobaldi (Fig. 47).

A somewhat younger contemporary of Frescobaldi was the German, Samuel Scheidt, who was born at Halle in 1587, almost one hundred years before Bach. He is frequently called "the father of German organ music," a designation which may be challenged by pointing to the great German organ composer, Arnolt Schlick, who lived one hundred years before Scheidt. It is true, however, that Scheidt is the initial link in that uninterrupted succession of outstanding organ composers of whom Bach is the last. Scheidt was one, in fact the most important, of the numerous pupils of Sweelinck, from whom he adopted, among other things, the figural keyboard style and the variation technique of the English virginalists. On the whole, Scheidt lacks the ingenious imagination of his teacher. His variations would seem to be to those of Sweelinck as life and cultural conditions in the provincial town of Halle were to those in the metropolitan city of Amsterdam. Never-

47. FRESCOBALDI—*Canzona*

theless, the basic simplicity and introspective seriousness of the German small-town musicians like Scheidt and many others, including Bach, proved, in the long run, a more valuable asset than the versatility of composers living in London, Venice, Amsterdam, or Rome. Scheidt's style may be illustrated here (Fig. 48) by some of his twelve variations on a *Cantio Belgica* (Belgian song) called "Wehe, Windgen, Wehe" (Blow, Wind, Blow).

We now turn to the third country in which keyboard music flourished during the seventeenth century: France. Here Jacques Champion de Chambonnières (1602?–1672?) holds a position comparable to that of Scheidt, for he also was the first in a series of brilliant keyboard composers—in his case a series which culminated with Bach's contemporary, Jean Philippe Rameau (1683–1764). Aside from this, however, French keyboard music, from its inception, presents a picture entirely different from that encountered in Italy or Germany. While Frescobaldi was in the employment of the Pope, and Scheidt was organist of a small-town Protestant church, Chambonnières worked at Versailles, as court musician to Louis XIV. He did not care to write for the service of the Church, or to puzzle over the problems of counterpoint. His sole aim and purpose was the entertainment of the court society whose interest, as far as music was concerned, was practically confined to dance music until, later, the opera came to Paris. Therefore, Chambonnières as well as the later clavecinists devoted themselves almost exclusively to the composition of music modeled after dance types. Chambonnières' dances are largely the same which prevail in suites of Bach, that is, allemandes, courantes, sarabandes, and gigues. As might well be expected in the surroundings in which they grew up, these compositions combine exquisite refinement with measured dignity. A specially beautiful trait, to be found particularly in the allemandes, is the extended flow of the musical phrase. Like Gibbons in his pavane, Chambonnières frequently carries the musical thought considerably farther than the commonplace scheme of the four-measure phrase demands. The same tendency toward continuity can be seen in the harmonic structure which often

·92·

shows unexpected modulations instead of the normal cadential endings. A beautiful example of this style exists in his "Allemande la Rare," the beginning of which is something like that shown in Fig-

48. SCHEIDT—*Wehe, Windgen, Wehe*

1. Variatio.

2. Variatio.

3. Variatio.

4. Variatio.

12. Variatio.

ure 49. Actually, Chambonnières avoids the orthodox close with the full cadence and, in a most impressive manner, carries on the melodic as well as the harmonic motion as illustrated in Figure 50.

49.

50.

Chambonnières' compositions are, of course, expressly written for the harpsichord or, as the French called it, clavecin. A typical trait of the French harpsichord style is the numerous ornamentations, such as trills, mordents, and appoggiaturas. Prejudiced writers of the nineteenth century, in a characteristic attitude of condescending indulgence, have explained these ornamentations as an expedient to overcome certain deficiencies of the harpsichord, particularly its supposed incapacity for sustained sound. Actually, the sustaining power of the harpsichord is hardly less than that of the pianoforte. But aside from this fact, the ornamentations of French Baroque music, far from being an external decoration which may be better omitted, are an integral feature of the musical style. True enough, they are not part of

51. CHAMBONNIÈRES—*Allemande la Rare*

the main structure, of the basic texture—they are only an embroidery. But the word "only" is out of place. This a Frenchman will readily understand, though it may be more difficult to appreciate for the puristic mind of the Englishman, or for the abstract mind of the German. Chambonnières' "Allemande la Rare" (Fig. 51) may serve as an illustration of French harpsichord style around 1650.

The most outstanding among the numerous pupils of Chambonnières is Jean Henri d'Anglebert (1628?–1691) who, like his teacher, was court clavecinist to Louis XIV. Although little known today, he represents the highest development of French harpsichord music, even more so than François Couperin who is usually considered the most outstanding of the clavecinists. In fact, Couperin's pieces, charming though they are, are not free from a certain facile pleasingness which indicates the decline of Baroque art and the beginning of Rococo style. In d'Anglebert, however, the loftiness and grandeur of Baroque mentality found a most impressive realization, equal in artistic significance to that of the other outstanding masters of the period. In regard to form as well as style he carried on the tradition of Chambonnières. The qualities to be admired in his compositions are essentially the same as those we found in Chambonnières, but developed and refined to the highest degree of mastery. D'Anglebert's "Allemande" in G-minor (Fig. 52) is an impressive example of this truly great art.

Dance types such as the allemande and sarabande played a considerable role in Baroque music because they became the constituent members of one of the most important forms of the period, the suite. The history of the suite is a very interesting one. It may be briefly outlined here since it lends itself better to summary description than does the development of many other musical forms. According to definition, the suite is a composite instrumental form consisting of a number of movements, each in the character of a dance, and all in the same key. In the interest of clarity it may be advisable to start with a description of the suite in the final stage of its development, as represented by Bach. Bach's suite can be characterized by the scheme: A–C–S–O–G.

52. D'Anglebert—*Allemande*

Here A stands for allemande, C for courante, S for sarabande, G for gigue, and O for what is called optional dance or optional group, that is, one or several dances of various types, chiefly the minuet, bourrée, gavotte, passepied, polonaise, rigaudon, and anglaise. For instance, one of Bach's French Suites consists of the following eight movements: Allemande, Courante, Sarabande, Gavotte, Polonaise, Bourrée, Minuet, Gigue. Turning to a consideration of the development leading to Bach's suites one encounters an interesting picture of international coöperation. Briefly stated, Italy contributed the basic idea of combining several dances into a larger unit, England produced the gigue, Spain the sarabande, France a great wealth of other dance types, and Germany not only the allemande but, more important, the conception of the suite as a unified and definite musical form. As regards the primitive Italian suite of the sixteenth century, it will suffice to mention combinations such as passemezzo–gagliarda–padovano or passamezzo–padovano–saltarello–ripresa which occur in the Italian lute books of about 1540. Towards the end of the sixteenth century there developed those new dances which were to become the standard members of the Baroque suite: the allemande, the courante, the sarabande, and the gigue. Extensive collections of these dances occur in lute and harpsichord books of French composers of the early Baroque period, such as Jean-Baptiste Besard, Chambonnières, Louis Couperin (an uncle of François Couperin), d'Anglebert, and others. Although in these collections the arrangement of the dances is to some extent the same as in the classical suite, beginning with the allemande, following up with the courante, and so on, the idea of the suite as a definite musical form is lacking. For instance, Besard's lute book of 1603 falls into different *livres* (sections), the first of which contains all the allemandes, the second, all the courantes, and so forth, in various keys. Chambonnières' dances, as found in the earliest source, a manuscript of about 1650,[24] are arranged according to keys, but in such large numbers as to exclude the idea of a definite form. For instance, the C-major group of this manuscript consists of 5 allemandes, 11 courantes, 4 sarabandes, 2 gigues, 5 courantes, and 1 chaconne. Chambonnières' successors reduced these accumulations to smaller numbers and, eventually, to a single representative of each form, but pursued the trend towards a loose aggregation of free types rather than towards a standard arrangement. This trend found its fullest realization in the suites —if they can thus be called—of François Couperin, which rarely include an allemande, courante, or sarabande, but consist mostly of a succession of descriptive pieces with titles such as "Les Bergeries" (The Shepherds), "Le Moucheron" (The Mosquito), and "Les Moissonneurs" (The Reapers).

To the best of our knowledge, the creation of the suite as a fixed musical form was the work of a German composer of the mid-seventeenth century, Johann Jakob Froberger (1616–1667). With him the suite started out as a three-movement form, allemande–courante–sarabande. Other suites of Froberger, possibly of a slightly later date, include the gigue, but this appears either before or after the courante, with the sarabande retaining its position as the concluding movement: A–C–G–S or A–G–C–S. Practically all the suites written before about 1690 follow one of these patterns which reserve the slow and expressive sarabande for the concluding movement, thus bestowing upon the early suite a tinge of Romanticism which is not infrequent in Baroque music. It was not until after Froberger's death that the gigue became established as the final movement. This fact becomes clear from a comparison of Froberger's suites as they appear in his autographic manuscripts with those of the first printed edition which was published in 1693, sixteen years after his death. While the former source shows them in the arrangements indicated above, they are re-arranged in the latter so that the gigue forms the final movement. This change, leading to the scheme A–C–S–G, is expressly referred to in the title of the printed edition by the remark *mis en meilleur ordre* (put in better order). Better or not, the new arrangement of the four standard dances became universally adopted toward the end of the seventeenth century.

At about the same time we find the earliest examples of the suites including an optional dance, for instance, those by Krieger of 1697

53. FROBERGER—*Suite*

Allemande.

·102·

Courante.

Sarabande.

which show the arrangement A–C–S–G–O, or those by Pachelbel, of 1699, with the scheme A–C–O–S–G. It seems that Bach was the first and, for that matter, almost the only composer to place the optional dance before the gigue, in the well-known arrangement A–C–S–O–G which formed the point of departure of our brief survey.

After this excursion dealing with the development of the suite we may return to its originator, Froberger. One of his three-movement suites is reproduced here (Fig. 53) as an illustration of the point of departure of this form. This composition also serves to illustrate Froberger's style, which, in comparison with that of other composers of his day, is unusually sensitive and delicate.

Froberger is one of the very few among the earlier composers whose personality is of distinct interest from the musical point of view. In fact, it is in his works that for the first time we can occasionally sense the expression of personal feelings. A crossing of the channel in adverse weather, an unfriendly welcome in a foreign city, or the death of a beloved friend so much impressed his sensitive mind that he expressed his feelings in music—a reaction which was just as unusual in the seventeenth and eighteenth centuries as it was common with the Romantic composers of the nineteenth century. A most beautiful example of Froberger's Romanticism exists in his "Lamentation faite sur la mort tres douloureuse de Sa Majestè Imperiale, Ferdinand le troisieme" (Lament on the most grievous decease of his Imperial Majesty, Ferdinand the Third). Such laments, or as the French called them, *tombeaux* (tombstones) or *plaintes* (plaints), were by no means uncommon in early Baroque music. Particularly in France it was almost customary for a composer to write a tombeau on the death of his teacher, or of a close friend. Thus, Louis Couperin as well as d'Anglebert wrote a tombeau for Chambonnières, and François Couperin wrote tombeaux for Lully and Corelli. While these composi-

Lamentation faite sur la mort tres douloureuse de Sa Majesté Imperiale, Ferdinand le troisome; et se joue lentement avec discretion. An. 1657.

tions usually show a somewhat traditional expression of dignified sorrow without permitting personal feelings to come to the fore, Froberger's "Lamentation" (Fig. 54) has a much more individual character. Here it is not a tradition that expresses itself, but a man and an artist—a man who feels and an artist who transmutes the feeling. In its true expression of a genuine feeling this composition is as typically German—and, for that matter, as typically Romantic—as a Träumerei by Schumann, or an Intermezzo by Brahms. Among the many remarkable traits of Froberger's compositions' musical language, the impressive recitative and the bold harmonies may be mentioned, as well as, particularly, the ascending broken chords of the last measure in which the redeemed soul of the deceased rises to heaven.

5

1675 — THE LATE BAROQUE PERIOD — 1750

IN THE PRECEDING CHAPTER we considered the most outstanding keyboard composers of the early Baroque period: the Italian Frescobaldi, the French Chambonnières and d'Anglebert, the German Scheidt and Froberger. It may be noticed that, while Chambonnières and d'Anglebert are successive members of one and the same musical school, located in Paris, Scheidt and Froberger represent two widely different lines of development, as far removed one from another as were their places of life and work. As is well known, cultural life in Germany has always been decentralized, particularly in those days when Germany consisted of a multitude of small sovereign states, each with its own center of culture. However this situation may be assessed from the political point of view, it produced most beneficial results in all the fields of intellectual and artistic life, leading to a prolification and dissemination for which there is no parallel in any other country. The German music of the Baroque period, particularly of its second half, clearly reflects this situation. Out of the destruction wrought by the Thirty-Years War (1618–1648) there arose, in an almost miraculous way, a wealth of musical life, so abundant that it cannot be properly considered under the single classification of "German music." At least three different lines of evolution must be distinguished, a South-German, a Middle-German, and a North-German. The South-German composers worked mainly in Vienna and Munich, the North-German, in Hamburg and Lübeck, the Middle-German, in Nuremberg and in the numerous small towns of Thuringia in which Bach's ancestors lived and worked.

The composers of South Germany were strongly under the influence of Frescobaldi, an influence which appears in their cultivation of the strict contrapuntal forms like the ricercar or the canzone, and which led to a somewhat formalistic conservatism. Perhaps as a relief, they occasionally resorted to musical jokes, in the then current style of program music. Easily the most attractive of these is a series of variations, "Aria Allemagna con alcuni Variazoni" (Fig. 55) , by Alessandro Poglietti, an Italian who worked in Vienna and died there in 1681, during the Turkish siege. Poglietti wrote these variations in 1677, as a birthday present for the ruling Austrian empress, Eleonora Maddalena Theresa, representing through their number—like so many candles on a birthday cake—the age of his august patroness. Fortunately, the empress was only twenty years old, young enough so that her age could be revealed without being impolite to her, and without overstraining the patience of the audience. Most of these variations are based on programmatic ideas indicated by titles such as: "Lyra," "Böhmisch Dudlsack" (Bohemian Bagpipe) , "Ungarische Geigen" (Hungarian Fiddles) , "Bayrische Schalmay" (Bavarian Shawm) , "Französische Baiselemans" (French Kiss-the-Hand) , "Gaugler Seiltanz" (Juggler's Rope-dance) , "Alter Weiber Conduct" (Old Hag's Procession) , "Hanacken Ehrentantz" (Dance of the Honor-guard) , and so on. Although not of a very refined taste, these pieces are amusing portrayals of topics gathered from the various provinces of the sprawling Austrian Empire, thus forming a motley pageant in honor of the young empress.

In turning to North Germany we encounter an entirely different picture, a picture characterized by native rather than foreign traits, by freedom of thought rather than conservatism, by boldness of imagination rather than academic rigidity. True enough, the point of departure of this development is indicated by the Dutchman Sweelinck, whose numerous German pupils open the long series of North-German organists; but what "foreign" elements may have existed in his music were easily assimilated and transformed into a genuine German style, as may well be expected in view of the close cultural relationship between the Netherlands and northern Germany. After all, the North-German musicians did not have to cross the Alps in order to find teachers.

The development of North-German organ music is indicated by men like Heinrich Scheidemann (1596?–1663), Franz Tunder (1614–1667), Matthias Weckmann (1621–1674), Johann Adam Reinken (1623–1722), Dietrich Buxtehude (1637–1707), Vincent Lübeck (1654–1740), Georg Böhm (1661–1733), and Nikolaus Bruhns (1665–1697). Among these Buxtehude is the most outstanding, but Tunder, Weckmann, Böhm, and Bruhns are also composers of high artistic significance.

The favored forms of the North-German school were the prelude and the toccata. The preludes of Scheidemann are interesting because they usually close with a section in fugal style, after an opening section in free prelude style. Thus they indicate the point of departure leading to the combination of prelude and fugue, well-known through Bach's *Well-tempered Clavier*. It was, however, in the toccata that the North-German organ music found its most characteristic and most impressive realization. In a striking contrast to Frescobaldi's multi-sectional toccatas, those of the North-German school—as well

55. POGLIETTI—*Aria Allemagna con alcuni Variazoni*

Parte 2da

Parte 8va. Böhmisch: Dudlsackh.

Parte 13^a. Alter Weiber Conduct.

Parte 14ª Hanacken Ehrentantz.

as those of Bach—usually follow the form of Merulo's toccatas, that is, they consist of three or five extended sections, alternating in free and fugal style. Thus, they also represent an extension of the principle embodied in the combination of a prelude with a fugue. As a matter of fact, the title *Praeludium cum Fuga* was frequently used for compositions which actually consist of two fugues enframed by three sections in free, improvisatory style—a prelude, an interlude, and a postlude.

A comparison of a toccata by Buxtehude (Fig. 56) with one of Merulo offers a most instructive illustration of a fundamental principle of musical development: conservatism of form combined with innovation of style. One and the same ground plan, as it were, is used as a foundation of two entirely different structures, one showing the broad and massive contours of the Renaissance, the other, the fantastic and visionary shapes of what one is tempted to call "Baroque Gothic." In fact, although they are typical products of Baroque music, these North-German toccatas show traits of a mentality which has frequently been likened to the transcendentalism of the late Gothic. Towering dimensions are filled with visions of sound as varied as the colors of a stained-glass window; with formations as free and fantastic as the Gothic gargoyles; with a feeling of unbounded exultation kindred to that which expressed itself in the cathedrals of the thirteenth century.

More than any other type of early keyboard music the North-German toccata depends for its realization on the resources of the Baroque organ with its limitless variety of strange and rigid timbres, with its tonal language of mystic excitation. The sound of the pianoforte is only a poor substitute for these sonorities, and it is only by combining his sense of hearing with his power of imagination that the reader may expect to obtain an adequate impression from a rendition on the pianoforte.

In addition to the toccata, the North-German composer cultivated the organ chorale, that is, organ compositions based on German Protestant Church hymns. Such compositions are usually known as chorale

·115·

preludes, a name which refers to the fact that they were used in the church service as a prelude preceding the singing of the hymn by the congregation. The term organ chorale, however, has the advantage of admitting the inclusion of the earlier examples of the Roman Catholic service, examples which, although similar in kind, did not serve as preludes to congregational singing, but were performed in the place of liturgical chants.

The development of the organ chorale goes back to at least the beginning of the sixteenth century. Compositions such as Arnold Schlick's "Salve Regina" or "Maria zart," which were discussed in Chapter 3, belong to the same general category, except for the fact that they are based on melodies of the Roman Catholic, not the German Protestant, liturgy. The Catholic organ chorale was by no means restricted to Germany. Numerous composers of the sixteenth century, like the English Redford, the Italian Cavazzoni, and the Spaniard Cabezón, wrote pieces of this type. After 1550, however, this activity declined in the Catholic countries, and among the Reformed Churches that of Germany was the only one to continue the tradition. There are several reasons for the marked difference in this matter between Germany and, for instance, England. The English Reformation established the psalter as practically the only source which was to supply the service with texts for congregational singing. Texts not drawn from the Bible were rejected as not being "inspired," and it was not until about 1700 that hymns gradually found their way into the worship. Luther took a much more liberal attitude in this matter. In his search for suitable texts he resorted chiefly to the Latin hymns of the Roman Church, many of which he, or his collaborators, translated into German. For instance, the ancient Latin hymn, "Veni redemptor gentium," written about 400 by St. Ambrose, became the German chorale "Nun komm, der Heiden Heiland" (Now come, the Gentiles' saviour) . As for the melodies, he freely borrowed from folk songs, French chansons, German love songs, or from other secular sources, providing them with a new text. The other important difference between the English and the German Reformation was that Luther did not banish the organ, but rather encouraged its use during the service. By these steps he provided the basis for the development of the Protestant organ chorale which was to become one of the most beautiful flowerings of Baroque art. Naturally, in the Lutheran Church the organ chorale held a position quite different from that which it occupied in the Roman service. In the latter the organ chorale served as a substitute for the plainsong, from which it inherited a definite liturgical function as well as that spirit of mystic aloofness and transcendence which pervades the whole Roman Catholic ritual. In the Protestant Church the singing of the chorale became the cherished privilege of the congregation, and it was the organist's duty not only to accompany this singing, but also to play the chorale beforehand on the organ, a procedure by which it adopted the extra-liturgical function of a chorale prelude.

The establishment of the German-Protestant chorale prelude proved a great stimulus to organ composition, and many new forms and methods grew up from this fertile ground. The chorale was no longer mysteriously concealed as a structural tenor in incomprehensibly long notes; it was made to stand out as a real melody in the soprano, recognizable to every member of the congregation. This was a method of composition of which Schlick's "Maria zart" was an early but isolated example. It must be noted, however, that the earlier methods of treatment were continued alongside the more recent methods, and that in Bach the two oldest types, the *cantus-firmus* chorale and the chorale motet, still represent the most elaborate manner of composition.

The term *cantus-firmus* chorale denotes a treatment in which the chorale appears in one voice only, usually tenor or bass, and in long equal note values, for instance each note occupying a whole measure. This type is by far the oldest of all chorale methods, going back into forms of composition developed in the twelfth century; Schlick's "Salve Regina" is an example of this type. The chorale motet developed in the sixteenth century from the model of the vocal motet from which it adopted the principle of successive "points of imitation," each point representing a short fugal treatment of a short phrase of literary text. Consequently, the chorale motet consists of several sections, each of which presents one of the successive lines of the chorale in imitative counterpoint. In the seventeenth century there developed other types of organ chorale. Particularly frequent are the melody chorale—in which the chorale tune appears in the soprano as a clearly perceptible melody, accompanied by contrapuntal parts in the lower voice; and the ornamented chorale—in which the original melody also occurs in the soprano, but enriched by expressive ornamentations. Other types are the chorale fugue, the chorale canon, and the chorale fantasia. The chorale fugue employs the imitative style of the chorale motet but, like the fugue, uses only one theme which is derived from the opening phrase of the chorale melody. In the chorale canon the melody appears in two voice parts in close imitation, after the fashion of a canon (or round). In the chorale fantasia the chorale melody is treated in a free, fanciful style, almost in the character of an improvisation.

As may well be expected, the last-mentioned type was especially favored in the North-German composers. Tunder, Buxtehude, Böhm, and Bruhns wrote chorale fantasias of great beauty, as did also, of course, Bach. Unfortunately, as in the case of the toccata, these extended compositions defy rendition on any instrument other than the Baroque organ. We must, therefore, be content with a more modest, but no less beautiful example of the North-German organ chorale, Buxtehude's "Durch Adams Fall ist ganz verderbt" (Through Adam's

57.

58.

59. BUXTEHUDE—*Durch Adams Fall ist ganz verderbt*

SECONDO

·120·

Duet Arranged by W. A.

PRIMO

·121·

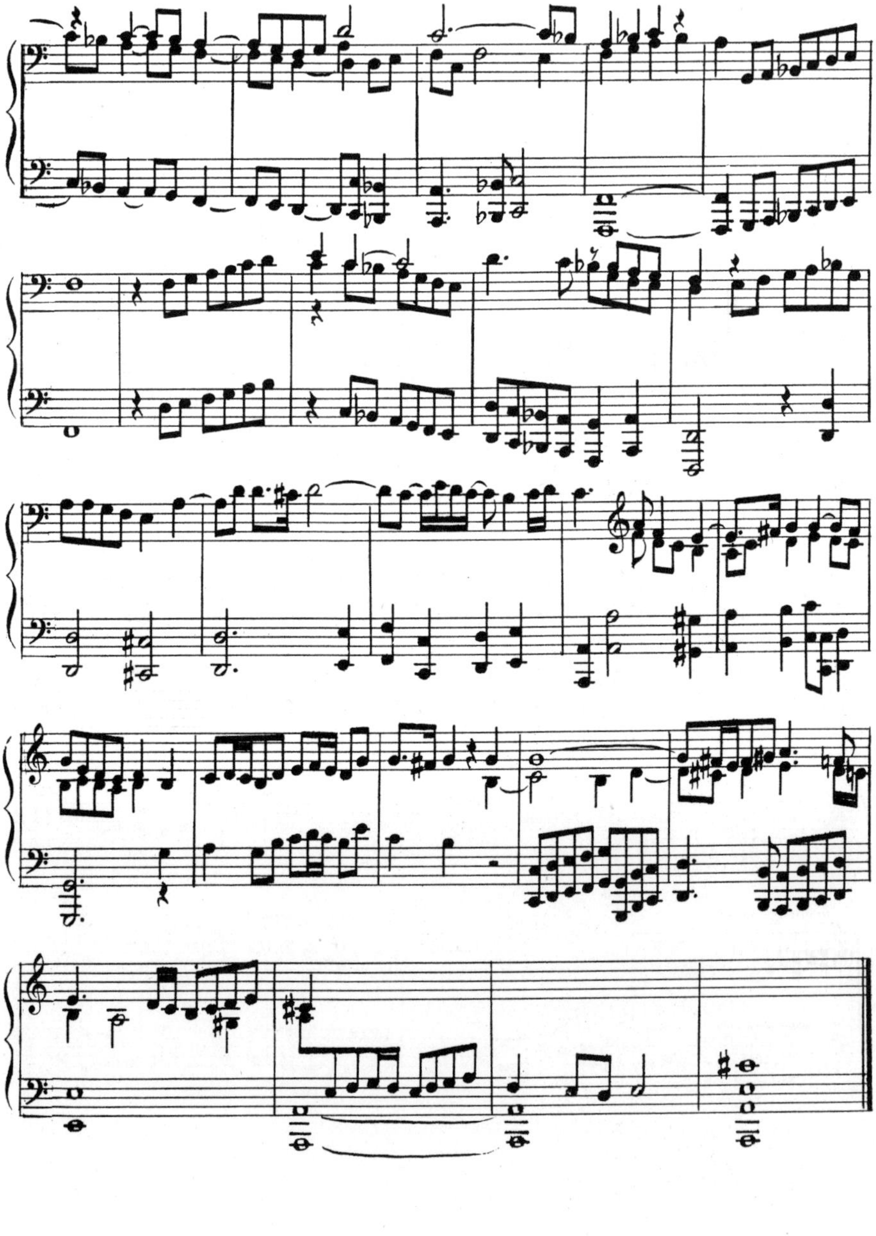

PRIMO

fall came our sin). This is chiefly in the character of a melody chorale, with the tune standing out clearly in the upper voice. The different lines of the chorale are separated by short interludes to be played on softer stops, and frequently the end of a line is put into relief by highly expressive coloraturas. For instance, the second line (Fig. 57) is transformed into a melody which is a truly Baroque gesture of ardent desire (Fig. 58). Buxtehude's composition is reproduced here (Fig. 59) in an arrangement for piano duet.

We finally turn to a consideration of the Middle-German school, localized mainly in Thuringia and in the northern, then Protestant, part of Bavaria of which Nuremberg is the center. In contrast to the learned ostentation of the South and the fantastic imagery of the North, the Middle-German composers inclined toward modesty of means and simplicity of style. Typical small-town musicians, they none the less succeeded through artistic integrity and seriousness of purpose. Their line is fittingly opened by Bach's great-uncle, Heinrich Bach (1615–1692), and his sons Johann Christoph Bach (1642–1703) and Johann Michael Bach (1648–1694), and it continues with the Nuremberg masters Johann Krieger (1652–1736) and Johann Pachelbel (1653–1706), and the Saxon composer Johann Kuhnau (1660–1722). Although the few organ pieces of the older Bachs which have been preserved are not particularly important, it may be interesting to include in this book a chorale prelude written by Heinrich Bach. His "Erbarm dich mein" (Fig. 60) is an example of the chorale fugue, a form which was particularly favored by the Middle-German composers owing to its shortness and simplicity of style.

Johann Pachelbel's compositions for the harpsichord include variations and suites, while for the organ he composed a considerable number of chorale preludes and pieces in fugal form. Most of these compositions show a simplicity of style and modesty of expression which, although not without charm, occasionally borders on provincial complacency. They represent a typically Middle-German branch of Baroque art, that art which found a similar expression in the churches and sculptures of the region. Pachelbel's suites are historically inter-

60. H. BACH—*Erbarm dich mein*

Ped.

esting since among them we find some of the earliest examples showing the addition of an optional dance to the four standard movements of allemande, courante, sarabande, and gigue (Fig. 61). It is interesting to notice that the optional dances of these suites are markedly different in style from the others, their musical texture being less elaborate and their melody and rhythm being more clearly in the character of real dance music. This difference, which can be noticed in all the suites of this period, including those by Bach, is conditioned by the historical development of the various dance types. As we have seen, the allemande, courante, sarabande, and gigue all originated late in the sixteenth century. When they were adopted into the suite they had already lost their dance connotation and had become idealized types, rhythmically weakened but artistically intensified. The optional dances, on the other hand, appeared almost one hundred years later, in the ballets of the court of Versailles where they had been brought from the various provinces of France. At the time of their adoption into the suite they were still in vogue and, therefore, largely retained their dance character.

Another important composer of the Middle-German group is Johann Kuhnau, Bach's predecessor at the St. Thomas Church in Leipzig. In 1692 Kuhnau published, under the title of *Neuer Clavier Uebung Andrer Theil,* a number of pieces for the harpsichord among which is a "Sonata aus dem B" (Sonata in B-flat), and it is on this composition that his chief fame as "inventor of the piano sonata" rests.

61. PACHELBEL—*Suite*

Courant.

Ballett.

Sarabanda.

Gyque.

Actually, this title is not wholly deserved. Five years before Kuhnau's book, the Italian composer Gregorio Strozzi had published, in his *Capricci da sonare cembali et organi* (1687), three pieces entitled "Sonata per cembali et organi"; sonatas written by Bernardo Pasquini (1637–1710) are quite possibly of an even earlier date. Even disregarding these Italian precedents (of which Kuhnau very likely had no knowledge), the term "inventor" is somewhat out of place, since Kuhnau's sonatas—written, to be sure, for the harpsichord, not the pianoforte—are nothing new in form or style; they are closely modeled after the violin sonatas of Legrenzi and Corelli. Thus Kuhnau only transferred a well-established form to a new medium, a procedure which can hardly be termed an "invention."

However the question of priority in this matter may be answered, there can be no disagreement about the artistic value of Kuhnau's sonatas: they are extremely dull and monotonous. He was, however, much more successful when, shortly after, he hit upon the idea of using the sonata as a vehicle of program music in such a manner that each movement would portray a scene or a chapter of a continuous narrative. In 1700 he published his *Musikalische Vorstellung einiger biblischen Historien* (Presentation of Sundry Biblical Stories), in which stories such as "The Combat between David and Goliath," "The Marriage of Jacob," or "Saul's Melancholy Cured by Music" are described in detail and, certain reservations notwithstanding, with considerable success. The beginning of the last sonata, a vivid and impressive description of Saul's melancholy and insanity, is given in Figure 62 as an illustration.

As a conclusion of our survey of German keyboard music before Bach, a composer must be mentioned who represents yet another branch of German Baroque music. This is Johann Kaspar Ferdinand Fischer (*c.* 1650–1746), who lived and worked in the southwestern part of Germany as a court conductor to the Margrave of Baden. The proximity of this court to France easily accounts for the strong French influence which is noticeable in Fischer's music. However, he never permitted this influence to take full possession of his musical person-

62. KUHNAU—*Saul Malinconico*

La tristezza ed il furore del Rè.

ality; rather he represents a happy amalgamation of French refinement and German solidity. The French influence is particularly conspicuous in his suites which, for the most part, discard the traditional standard types—except for the allemande—and consist mainly of the more recent ballet dances. For instance, one of his suites consists of prelude, allemande, passepied, rondeau, chaconne, gigue, bourrée, and two minuets; another of prelude, passacaille, bourrée, and minuet. As we have seen, the German composers of suites usually contented themselves with just a sprinkling of these novel ballet dances, as an element of variety within a traditional form. It may be noticed, however, that Bach, although usually adhering to the traditional type, also wrote several "ballet suites," as they may be called; these are his three orchestral suites and the so-called *French Overture* for the harpsichord, a magnificent composition which is actually an overture (in other words, introduction) in French style followed by a courante, two gavottes, passepied, sarabande, two bourrées, gigue, and echo.

Fischer's suites are among the earliest to have a prelude preceding the dance movements. These preludes are true gems of miniature art. Within twenty or thirty measures a little musical motive is fully exploited, the harmony is modulated and brought back to its beginning, and all the voices are introduced in polite, yet serious conversation; the whole is a truly admirable exhibition of craftsmanship and imagination within a small frame. The second of the two suites mentioned above, consisting of prelude, passacaille, bourrée, and minuet, is reproduced here (Fig. 63) as an example.

The tendency toward miniature forms is even more striking in Fischer's preludes and fugues which he published, in 1695, under the allegorical title of *Ariadne musica*, with reference to the Ariadne of Greek mythology who helped Theseus find his way out of the labyrinth. Fischer's musical labyrinth is the multitude of the major and minor keys; at that time the number of keys was just beginning to exceed the five or six simplest. Fischer wrote a prelude and fugue in nineteen keys, omitting only C-sharp major, E-flat minor, F-sharp major, A-flat minor, and B-flat minor of the complete system of twenty-

63. FISCHER—*Suite*

Praeludium

Passacaille.

Bourrée.

Menuet.

·135·

four. Thus, his *Ariadne* is an important forerunner of Bach's *Well-tempered Clavier* in which for the first time the cycle of all the keys was completed. Fischer's preludes and fugues rarely exceed the limit of twenty measures, but within this small frame they are no less complete and satisfactory than the dances of his suites. The second piece of the *Ariadne,* in C-sharp minor, serves as an example (Fig. 64).

We finally come to the incomparable culmination of Baroque music represented by Johann Sebastian Bach. Beethoven once said: "Nicht

64. FISCHER—*Prelude and Fugue*

Bach, Meer sollte er heissen"—a pun which rests on the literal meaning of the German word *Bach*, that is, brook—"Not brook, ocean
should be his name." A truly prophetic remark, the full significance
of which extends much beyond what Beethoven could possibly have
imagined. Beethoven was one of the first composers to draw from the
ocean of Bach's music: witness the great fugues which occur in his late
piano sonatas, and the ingenious counterpoint of his late string quartets. He may have felt certain that his successors would also turn to
the works of Bach as a source of inspiration, as indeed they did to
some extent. But Beethoven could not possibly have foreseen the tremendous influence which Bach was to exercise one hundred years
after these words were spoken, for today after so much confusion and
experimentation, composers have found new hope and confidence in
the motto "Back to Bach." Nor did Beethoven realize how valid his
simile was in its fuller sense, for the ocean is not only the inexhaustible
reservoir upon which to draw but also that into which all the brooks,
streams, and rivers flow. The recognition of this fact presupposes a
knowledge of pre-Bachian music which Beethoven could not have had.
Musicological research of the past fifty years, however, has clearly revealed Bach's position as the epitome and consummation of the efforts
of numerous earlier masters in many generations and different nations, a position which is entirely unique not only in the history of
music but, very likely, in that of all arts. Bach is indeed the crowning
keystone of the immense architecture of Baroque music. With an
amazing adaptability he absorbed the forms and styles of German,
French, and Italian music, and with incomparable mastery he brought
all of them to their culmination of artistic expression. Scheidt and
Frescobaldi, Buxtehude and Böhm, Pachelbel and Fischer, Couperin
and Vivaldi, all reappear in Bach, and in his late works, the *Musical
Offering* and the *Art of Fugue*, the tradition of the early Flemish masters of the fifteenth century, Ockeghem and Isaac, is brought to new
life.

Owing to this extraordinary influence of the past, Bach appears to us
as an extremely conservative figure, lacking to a large extent that qual-

ity which the modern mind considers an indispensable token of creative activity: originality. To put it more specifically, Bach's originality is that of a finisher, not of an innovator. While he raised every form and style of the past to the highest point of artistic perfection, he was completely uninterested in the novel tendencies of his time which indicated the breaking-away from the musical Baroque and which paved the way for the symphonies of Haydn and Mozart. Compared with Bach, Handel, who was born in the same year, was a progressive, and contemporaries like Telemann and Sammartini were radicals. It is perhaps Bach's conservatism which accounts for the fact that his work was not recognized by his contemporaries, particularly in the later period of his life. If he ever won universal acclaim, it was for his organ playing, not for his compositions, and the few who were impressed by his works nevertheless regarded them as old-fashioned and involved, as, in a way, they indeed were. When, upon the death of Kuhnau in 1722, the position of a cantor at St. Thomas in Leipzig became vacant it was first offered to Telemann, and it was only after he declined the offer, having much more lucrative positions in Hamburg, that the city council of Leipzig reluctantly chose Bach, stating in their proceeding that "none of the very best could be had." Even more astonishing is a sentence found in an article written four years after Bach's death,[25] in which the leading German composers of the day are listed in the following order: Hasse, Handel, Telemann, Johann Graun, Karl Graun, Stölzel, Bach, Pisendel, and Blümler. Today it seems all but incomprehensible that Hasse and Graun should be placed before Bach, and that such duly forgotten nonentities as Stölzel, Pisendel, and Blümler should even be mentioned in connection with him.

It goes without saying that only the barest outline of the scope and significance of Bach's keyboard compositions can be given here. Any selection that may be made for the purpose of illustration is, of course, not more than a fleeting glimpse into a vast treasure house filled with innumerable masterworks each of which deserves to be studied. The historical point of view, which is the guiding principle of this book, justifies and demands that particular consideration should be given to such compositions as most clearly illustrate Bach's position as the crowning keystone of Baroque music.

Starting with the fugue, it appears that the excellence of Bach's fugues over those of his predecessors results from various factors: greater contrapuntal skill, clarification of the formal structure, more advanced methods of harmonic treatment, and so on. While all these traits can be, and must be, understood as representing progress by degrees, there is one which puts Bach's fugues entirely into a class of their own, this is the incomparable artistic quality of their themes. In this respect, a comparison of the fugues in Bach's *Well-tempered Clavier* with those of its predecessor, Fischer's *Ariadne musica,* proves extremely illuminating. Such a comparison shows that Bach took over not only the general idea of a collection of preludes and fugues through all the twenty-four keys, but also certain fugal themes. For instance, the theme of Fischer's fugue in F-major reappears in Bach's fugue of the same key; reappears indeed, but in a modified shape which actually makes it something entirely different. Figure 65 shows the themes of the two fugues.

65.

The difference is indeed striking, more striking perhaps than the similarity. Two flaws can easily be singled out in Fischer's theme: first, the conspicuousness of its rhythmic design; and second, the fact that it comes to a full stop in the fourth measure. Both these traits mark it as a theme for a dance—for example, a gigue—rather than for a fugue. Bach, with his keen feeling for the intrinsic qualities of a fugue, avoids both these defects. The dotted rhythm of Fischer's theme is aban-

·139·

doned, and the full stop is replaced by a continuous flow which leads on without interruption. Another difference, of no less importance, appears if the two melodies are studied and compared with regard to their motion character. This term is meant to denote what may be called the geometrical design of a melody, as indicated by the higher or lower position of its notes on the musical staff. Such a design may be ascending or descending, it may consist of narrow steps of the scale or include leaps as in the tones of a broken chord, and so on. Theoretical and intellectual though such a consideration is likely to appear at first, it is of basic importance in the study of melody, a study which, by the way, is almost completely neglected although it is easily the most important field of aesthetic analysis in music. The importance of the approach through motion character is likely to become even more apparent if the musical graph is interpreted, as it should be, as the result of what may be called the physical forces of music. As a matter of fact, a melody is like a moving body which is subject to forces causing and regulating its motion. Perhaps the central concept of such a consideration is that of "musical gravity," a term which describes the fact that the natural movement of a musical line is downward, as is the natural moving of a body. Conversely, an ascending motion always has the character of tension and energy. In this respect it is interesting to note that the ancient Greeks invariably considered their scales as starting with the highest note and moving downwards, while the opposite interpretation, familiar to us, is an indication of the dynamic point of view which is characteristic of European music. In the light of these explanations, the comparative weakness of Fischer's theme, and the strength of Bach's is patent. Fischer's melody is essentially a descending scale (Fig. 66), and the dotted motive, also descending (Fig. 67), which is used in the first two measures, only serves to emphasize its fundamental feebleness, or, at the most, to conceal it under

66.

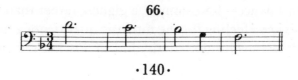

67.

the appearance of rhythmic vigor. Bach's theme, on the other hand, represents an admirable interplay of musical forces, descending and ascending in alternation, with each motion receiving, as it were, its elastic impetus from the opposite energy of the preceding motion.

These remarks should not lead to rash conclusions, for instance, that a melody in descending motion is bad, and that one in ascending motion is good. No such easy generalization is permissible in a field which, in spite of certain simple principles and premises, represents a highly complex and, for that reason, most interesting phenomenon. Nor should our point of view be construed as a system of measurement, as a yardstick which, if correctly applied, would indicate the artistic value of a melody in inches or percentages. Nor, finally, is it in any way a recipe of how to make good melodies or themes. To do this is the privilege, indeed the main criterion, of the musical genius. The nineteenth-century development of music, with its increasing emphasis on the exploitation of harmonies, of orchestral colors, and of rhythm as an independent factor, has temporarily obscured the fact that melody is not only the one element common to music of all times and races, but that it is the cornerstone and touchstone of artistic quality. Harmony, orchestration, and rhythm are based on certain rational premises which make them capable of being learned systematically; many composers of mediocre rank have, no doubt, been extremely adept at such studies and their practical application. Only the great artist, however, possesses that power of imagination and creation which goes into the making of a great melody. It is significant, as well as deplorable, that in the past fifty years hundreds of books on harmony and orchestration have been written and that courses in these subjects form an indispensable part of the curriculum of all our teaching institutions, while the study of melody is almost completely neglected.[26]

68. J. S. BACH—*Prelude and Fugue*

PRAELUDIUM

FUGA

After this excursion into a field on which we shall occasionally touch again, we return to Bach. To illustrate his incomparable mastery of fugal style I have reproduced the Prelude and Fugue in E-flat major (Fig. 68) from the second volume of the *Well-tempered Clavier*. As is well known, this title refers to the then novel method of tuning known as equal temperament (or well-tempered tuning) which is still used. This method made it possible to play equally well in all the keys, while in the earlier systems the simple keys were in more perfect tune, with the result that the keys with many sharps and flats could not be used at all. Bach was the first to make the practical application of the new method of tuning, in the two volumes of his *Well-tempered Clavier* (completed respectively *c.* 1722 and 1744), each of which consists of twenty-four preludes and fugues in all the twenty-four keys (twelve major and twelve minor), starting with C-major and ending with B-minor.

Bach's suites for keyboard consist mainly of three collections of six suites each, known as the English Suites, the French Suites, and the Partitas. It may be noticed that the first and the second of these terms are not only unauthentic but also devoid of significance, insofar as there are no specific English traits in the suites of the former set, nor French ones in those of the latter (aside from those French elements which are common to all the suites of German composers). The term partita, however, which is borrowed from Italian terminology, is authentic and does have significance insofar as these suites show Italian influence to some extent. The difference in style between the older and the more recent dance types which we observed in the suite by Pachelbel is even more patent in Bach's suites. His allemandes, courantes, sarabandes, and gigues are highly idealized types which are far removed from any dance connotation. His gavottes, bourrées, polonaises, and minuets, on the other hand, retain the characteristic traits of a dance, recreated through the interpretation of an imaginative artist. Five movements from the sixth of the French Suites serve as an illustration (Fig. 69).

Bach's chorale preludes form a treasure the significance of which is

69. J. S. BACH—*French Suite No. VI*

Allemande.

Polonaise.

far from being realized even by many of those musical amateurs familiar with the fugues and suites. No better means of introduction into the musical world of Bach can be found than these chorale preludes. Their variety of styles and procedures, conciseness of form, expressiveness of language, not to mention their supreme beauty and artistic greatness, give them a place within the compositions of Bach comparable to that held by the lyric poems within the writings of Goethe: that of a microcosmos in which the vast dimensions and overflowing thoughts of their large works are conveniently reflected. The fact that the chorale preludes are written for the organ prevents them from being played as extensively as the compositions for harpsichord or clavichord; but a number of them are available in piano transcriptions,[27] and most of them can very easily be performed with the aid of another player who simply plays the part for the organ pedal, doubling it in the lower octave.

Historically, Bach's chorale preludes represent the culmination of a development which started around 1500 with Arnolt Schlick, and which continued with men like Redford, Scheidt, Heinrich Bach, Buxtehude, and Pachelbel, to mention only a few names familiar to us. These musicians developed the various methods of chorale treatment which have been described previously and which Bach used with consummate skill and imagination. Two of his most beautiful organ chorales are reproduced here, both based on the Christmas song "In Dulci Jubilo." The first (Fig. 70) is essentially a melody chorale (the notes of the well-known carol are marked by crosses), but in addition an element of the free toccata style is introduced by the flowing passages which appear at the end of each line, connecting this with

70. J. S. BACH—*In Dulci Jubilo*

the next line and continuing there as a contrapuntal figuration. Throughout the composition there is an irresistible flow of motion, but the most dramatic moment comes when, with the entrance of the last line of the chorale, these sweeping forces are suddenly brought to halt, in a grandiose manifestation of a higher power which may well suggest the celestial hosts singing. Surely, never has the rejoicing spirit of Christmas found a more magnificent expression than in the triumphant flow of these passages and in the majestic splendor of these chords.

Our second example (Fig. 71) shows the same chorale differently treated, this time as a canon.[28] Its expression forms a striking contrast to that of the preceding example, reflecting, as it does, the idyllic scene of the adoration of the shepherds which has been so beautifully expressed in numerous pastorales and sicilianos of the Baroque masters. It is given here in an arrangement for piano duet.

I find it impossible to leave Bach without at least mentioning some of the many other great masterworks he contributed to our field. There is the *Chromatic Fantasia and Fugue,* the most impressive product of his youthful period, a work noticeable for its bold use of chromatic harmonies, anticipating by one hundred years the chromatic harmonies of Chopin (see p. 249). There is the *Italian Concerto,* a composition modeled after the violin concertos of contemporary Italian composers like Antonio Vivaldi, which in its clear and concise form, detached style, and restrained tension is the antipode to the rhapsodic peregrinations and dramatic outbursts of the Chromatic Fantasia. There are the numerous great organ works, such as the C-minor Passacaglia and D-minor Toccata and Fugue, which should be studied and, if possible, heard, in their original form, unadulterated by the sensationalism of modern orchestrators and film producers. There is, finally, his last work, the *Art of Fugue,* which, long considered as an unsurpassed manual of advanced counterpoint, has during the last two decades become recognized as one of the greatest creations of musical art. Unfinished, it breaks off suddenly at the point where for the first time the theme B–A–C–H is introduced —a deeply moving symbol of human life and eternity.

71. J. S. BACH—*In Dulci Jubilo*

SECONDO

·154·

PRIMO

1725 — THE ROCOCO PERIOD — 1775

THE MIDDLE OF THE EIGHTEENTH CENTURY is a little-known but extremely interesting period of music history. Like a hidden valley it lies between two towering mountain ranges: Bach and Handel on the one side, Haydn, Mozart, and Beethoven on the other. If one considers the fact that only forty years separate such utterly different masterworks as Bach's *Art of Fugue* and Mozart's *Jupiter Symphony,* he may well wonder how so fast a change from one high point to another was possible. In answer to this question two special traits in the evolutionary structure of eighteenth-century music must be considered: first, the fact that the development of Baroque music reached its zenith at the very close of the period; second, that the new development started a long time before it came to a clearly visible high point in Haydn and Mozart. In fact, traces of this development can be found as early as the beginning of the eighteenth century. It was at this time that a new style appeared in the fine arts which became known by the name Rococo, derived from the French word *rocaille* (shell-work). A true outgrowth of the luxury and sumptuousness of the court of Versailles, this style is characterized by an abundance of decorative scrolls and shell-work, by an emphasis on elegance and pleasingness, and amorous and frivolous subjects. The famous French painter Watteau, who was born one year before Bach, was one of its first champions. Watteau's musical counterpart is François Couperin, who was born in 1668, almost twenty years before Bach, and who published, between 1713 and 1730, four books called *Livres de pièces de clavecin.* These books indicated a definite break with the tradition of Baroque music, and inaugurated the period of the musical Rococo or, as it is frequently called, the "gallant style." Of all the forms of Baroque keyboard music, Couperin chose to concentrate on the suite. Not, to be sure, the suite of Froberger, Pachelbel, and Bach, but the type developed by Chambonnières, d'Anglebert, and the other French clavecinists, which consisted of a rather loose conglomeration of a multitude of pieces, held together only by the unity of key. In his first book, Couperin opens his suites or, as he calls them, *ordres,* with the three oldest dance types, allemande, courante, sarabande; these are followed by a number of pieces, in one case as many as fourteen, most of which are no longer modeled after dances, but are freely invented compositions with descriptive titles such as "Les Abeilles" (The Bees), "L'Enchanteresse" (The Enchantress), "Les Ondes" (The Waves), "Les Papillons" (The Butterflies), and so on. Others bear inscriptions such as "La Madeleine," "La Fleurie," "La Mimi," "La Garnier," evidently dedicatory titles of pieces meant to portray some characteristic trait of the person, presumably a lady of the court, for whom it was written. In the three later books, published in 1716, 1722, and 1730, the dance types, whether old or new, disappear completely, and the *ordres* now consist of five or six freely invented pieces, with descriptive or dedicatory titles. For instance, an *ordre* from the fourth book has the following pieces: "La Visionnaire" (The Visionary), "La Monflambert," "La Muse victorieuse" (The Victorious Muse), "Les Ombres errantes" (The Roaming Shadows).

The novelty of Couperin's procedure becomes even more apparant if matters of expression and style are considered. Charming and elegant, pleasing and trifling, graceful and amusing, his pieces represent an epoch in the history of music, because they indicate the breaking away from that basic attitude of dignified seriousness which theretofore had pervaded the entire music of the Baroque period, secular as well as sacred. With Couperin, music lost its religious affiliation and became solely a matter of entertainment: what had been a vocation by the grace of God became a profession by grace of the King of

France. From a long-range point of view this shift of allegiance—which, of course, found a similar expression in the other arts as well as in the literature of the period—was of the highest consequence. It paved the way for that later stage in which music became its own absolute sovereign, under Haydn, Mozart, Beethoven, and their successors. The fact should not be overlooked, however, that it also opened the door for a flood of mediocrity, banality, and vulgarity which started in the middle of the eighteenth century and which, to the present day, has continued to rise.

Finally, it may be mentioned that many harpsichord pieces by Couperin show a novel technique of composition: the use of a short, characteristic keyboard figure or motive as the basis of the entire piece, this motive being carried through from the beginning to the end by means of harmonic progressions and modulations; "Le Tic-Toc-Choc" (Fig. 72) illustrates his methods. It is interesting to notice that this

72. COUPERIN—*Le Tic-Toc-Choc*

technique also figures prominently in the piano compositions of Romantic composers like Schumann (e.g. "Novellette," op. 21, no. 2 —Fig. 73) and Chopin (e.g. "Prelude," op. 28, no. 1—Fig. 74).

73. SCHUMANN—*Novellette*—OP. 21, NO. 2

74. CHOPIN—*Prelude*—OP. 28, NO. 1

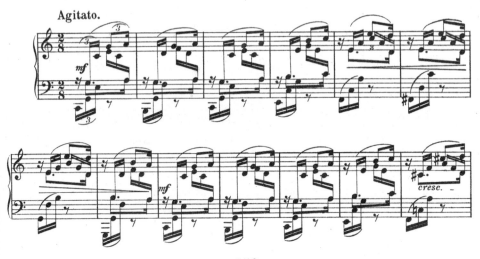

Among Couperin's pieces are numerous examples of program music, a category which was quite prominent in the Baroque era, although it is frequently considered an invention of the nineteenth century. Naturally, there is a wide difference between the program music of Couperin and that of, for instance, Franz Liszt, not only in matters

75. COUPERIN—*Le Rossignol en amour*

of style, expression, technical means, and so on, but also as regards the fundamental attitude towards the program, that is, the extra-musical idea on which the composition is based. Briefly stated, the early musicians took the programmatic idea much less seriously than do modern composers. While modern musicians aim at complete conformity between the program and the composition, the earlier composers used the program only as a point of departure from which they usually derived not much more than the general design of the initial theme. Moreover, while the modern program composition is prevailingly subjective, being concerned with portraying feelings and moods, the old composers concerned themselves mostly with portraying objective things, such as the cries of birds, the noise of a battle, the flight of an army, the running of a brook, the limping of cripples, and so on. Naturally, these features combine to make the early compositions much less interesting examples of program music than are those of the modern composers. But the artistic significance of program music in the modern sense of the word has been considerably overrated, and it is perhaps all to the good that, in the program pieces of the early composers, the emphasis is on the music, not on the program. Two examples may serve to illustrate Couperin's method: "Le Rossignol en amour"—The Nightingale in Love (Fig. 75) — and "La Distraite"—The Distracted (Fig. 76).

76. COUPERIN—*La Distraite*

Tendrement, et tres lié.

Couperin's successor in the field of French harpsichord music was Jean Philippe Rameau, born in 1683. In a way, Rameau is more truly a Baroque composer, less clearly a Rococo composer, than Couperin. There is a seriousness of purpose, a profundity of thought in his works which differs strikingly from the somewhat trifling pleasingness of Couperin and which, on the whole, makes him appear as a composer of higher rank and greater significance. Many of his compositions show traits of ingenuity, surprise, or dramatic sweep which remind one of Beethoven. Such traits will readily be noticed in his "Les Cyclopes" (Fig. 77), a composition named after the giant blacksmiths of Greek mythology. This work is a perfect example of the early type of program music, subtly incorporating, as it does, the programmatic idea into the musical texture without letting it take full possession. One other composer on the border line between Baroque and Rococo should be mentioned here: the Italian, Domenico Scarlatti (1685–1757). He devoted himself to the harpsichord with an exclusiveness for which Chopin's cultivation of the piano offers the only parallel, but in this limited field he attained a technical elegance and virtuosity which also may well be compared to those of Chopin. His musical personality presents an interesting contrast to that of Couperin. His compositions, of which well over three hundred are preserved, are entirely free from programmatic connotation; they have no "meaning" other than that of their musical form and design. While Couperin's pieces attract us through their intimate and lyrical charm, those of Scarlatti fascinate through their unemotional detachment, clear precision, and technical brilliance. Continuity of melody is frequently replaced by a mosaic-like design consisting of a succession of different and often repeated patterns, a procedure which bestows upon his music a somewhat static quality, in spite of all the fast motion which usually prevails from the beginning to the end. Among the various pianistic devices which he introduced, the use of wide leaps, sometimes over three octaves, and the crossing of the hands deserve special mention. The sonata reproduced here (Fig. 78) well illustrates Scarlatti's style.

77. RAMEAU—*Les Cyclopes*

Scarlatti's compositions are usually referred to as sonatas. It is not entirely clear whether this designation is authentic. At any rate, it should be noticed that it does not conform with the usual meaning of the term sonata. In the Baroque period, as well as in classical and modern music, sonata designates, not a single piece, like those by Scarlatti, but a composite form consisting of three or four pieces of contrasting character, called movements. As has been pointed out in

78. D. SCARLATTI—*Sonata*

one of the preceding chapters, the sonata developed, around 1650, out of the instrumental canzona, the *canzona da sonare* as it was called, by a process of separation and standardization which led, around 1675, to two clearly defined types of Baroque sonata, the *sonata da chiesa* (church sonata) and the *sonata da camera* (chamber sonata), both for small instrumental groups—for example, two violins, cello, and harpsichord. The *sonata da chiesa* normally consisted of four movements of contrasting speed, in the arrangement slow–fast–slow–fast, while the *sonata da camera* was more or less like a suite, consisting of movements such as preludio, allemanda, corrente, and giga.

While the Baroque sonata reached its perfection under men like Corelli, Bach, and Handel, there started, around 1725, a new development which, in the course of fifty years, led to an entirely different type of sonata—the classical sonata of Haydn, Mozart, Beethoven, and their successors. The study of this development is one of the most interesting problems of musical research, but at the same time one of the most difficult. To the present day, no comprehensive study of this important phase of music history exists. This lack results not just from negligence or want of interest on the part of musical scholars, but primarily from the exceptional complexity of the phenomenon. In fact, the change from the Baroque sonata to the classical sonata involves much more than the change from a four-movement scheme adagio–allegro–adagio–allegro to another four-movement scheme allegro–adagio–scherzo–allegro. It also involves changes of the formal structure of the single movement, for instance, from the continuous style and relatively unfixed schemes of the early movements to contrasting themes and such definite forms as sonata form, ternary form, theme with variations, or rondo form. Then there is the question of style, no doubt the most intricate problem of all. Here the development leading from the polyphonic texture of the Baroque sonata over the feeble and facile style of the Rococo to the dynamic expressiveness of the Viennese classics would have to be traced. Finally, it should be noticed that the classical sonata developed simultaneously in three parallel lines: as a composition for harpsichord or pianoforte, later frequently with the addition of a violin or flute; as a composition for four stringed instruments, in which case it was, and still is called string quartet; and as a composition for the orchestra, called symphony. It is, of course, impossible to summarize this complicated process in a few sentences or paragraphs. Regarding the evolution of form, it must suffice to say that the classical sonata started, around 1750, as a rather loose type consisting of two or three movements. Among the keyboard sonatas of Rococo composers like Giovanni Battista Sammartini (1700?–1775), Platti (born *c.* 1700), Baldassare Galuppi (1706–1785), Pietro Domenico Paradies (1710–1792), and Giovanni Rutini (1730–1797) we find schemes such as: allegro-minuetto; larghetto-allegro-minuetto; andantino-allegro-presto; allegro-andante-allegro, and so on. The introduction of the four-movement scheme, allegro-adagio-minuet-allegro, must be credited to the founder of the so-called Mannheim School, Johann Stamitz (1717–1757), who used it in all his symphonies and quartets. This four-movement scheme is found in nearly all the symphonies and quartets of Haydn and Mozart, while their piano sonatas are in three movements only. Beethoven adopted the four-movement scheme for the piano sonata, and replaced the minuet with the scherzo.

The rise of this new form was accompanied by a decisive change of style. Briefly stated, this change may be described as the transition from polyphonic to homophonic style, that is, from a texture consisting of two, three, or four different and individual melodic lines sounding simultaneously to one consisting of a single melodic line supported by full harmonies.[29] Figure 79 illustrates this important point, showing one tune (a) in two-voice polyphony (or counterpoint), (b) in three-voice polyphony, (c) in homophonic style with full chords, and (d) with the full chords replaced by broken-chord patterns. The last method, known as Alberti-bass, became particularly popular with the Rococo composers and was still frequently used by Haydn and Mozart in their piano sonatas.

It is easy to see that the novel method of accompanied melody meant a considerable simplification of musical style. When, around 1750,

79.

it became fully established it was hailed as the liberation from what was then considered "the useless fetters of counterpoint" and was extolled, in the words of a contemporary philosopher, as the *retour à la nature*. Actually, this simplification at first brought with it an appalling deterioration of the musical quality because it failed to produce an equivalent for what had been discarded. This equivalent should have been a new type of melody, vital and vigorous enough to make up for the loss of contrapuntal energy. A new type of melody did indeed emerge, but it arose chiefly from the desire to cater to the demands of a pleasure-seeking multitude of middle-class amateurs, a stimulus which opened a new and deplorable chapter in music history.

·175·

To Italian composers like Galuppi, Paganelli, Graziolo, and Rutini goes the doubtful honor of having discovered a new field for music, the "market" on which what is purported to be art is manufactured and sold like merchandise. While they still endeavored to put up at least the appearance of artistic decency, this pretense was completely discarded in England where composers as well as publishers strove to exploit the new market with a remarkable approximation of modern business methods. The drawing-rooms of the nineteenth and the dancing halls of the twentieth century have produced a host of successors who have been selling much the same product, only more attractively wrapped up.

The style of the Italian Rococo composers may be illustrated by the beginning of a sonata by Galuppi (Fig. 80), one of those pieces

80. GALUPPI—*Sonata*

which, unfortunately, form the major part of the various volumes that were published around 1900 under pretentious titles such as "The Early Masters of the Pianoforte."

The artistic mediocrity of the Italian Rococo composers should not, of course, prevent us from recognizing their historical significance. Their adoption of the sonata as the exclusive form of keyboard music and their experiments with the novel style of accompanied melody laid the foundation for a development which was to become one of the most splendid in all music history. These experiments, much as they missed the mark, pointed towards those qualities which we so greatly admire in the works of Haydn, Mozart, and Beethoven —the qualities of true expression and dynamic power. Although in the works of these later masters these two qualities are completely amalgamated into an artistic unity, they were separately evolved by two groups of earlier German composers, the "dynamic" and the "expressive." The "dynamic" group is known under the name of the Mannheim School, so called because its members were connected with the court orchestra of Mannheim in southwest Germany.[30] Under the leadership of Johann Stamitz they established a completely new and revolutionary style of orchestral music characterized, among other things, by the use of dynamic devices such as extended crescendos, unexpected fortes and fortissimos, allegro and presto speed, and also a novel type of theme which quickly and determinedly rises over a high range. Since they only wrote symphonies and chamber music, they must remain unconsidered here. Suffice it to say that Beethoven in writing a theme such as that of the first movement of his first piano sonata (Fig. 81) was directly indebted to the Mannheim composers.

81.

Turning now to the "expressive" group of pre-classical composers, we come to a school in eighteenth-century music which is closely allied to a broader cultural movement of the period, known under the German name of *Empfindsamkeit,* or sensibility. This movement was represented by literary men, painters, and musicians who, in response to Rousseau's teachings, tried to arrive at an expression of true and natural feelings, anticipating to some extent the Romanticism of the nineteenth century. Unfortunately, a rather rationalistic point of view, involving such things as a classification of human affections, hampered their imagination and prevented the movement from fully achieving its aims. Nevertheless, it represents an important trend in eighteenth-century mentality, and one without which neither Goethe nor Beethoven can be imagined.

In music, the sensitive style is chiefly represented by the two eldest sons of Johann Sebastian Bach: Wilhelm Friedemann (1710–1784) and Karl Philipp Emanuel (1714–1788). Wilhelm Friedemann Bach is mostly known as the hero of several novels and stories in which he is invariably portrayed as the prototype of the Bohemian artist, leading a dissolute life and ending in utter poverty and oblivion. Although most of this is mere gossip, it is probably true that he did not fully realize his outstanding possibilities. The relatively few compositions which have been preserved show him as a composer of great significance, perhaps the only one who was able to elevate the somewhat formalistic methods of the *empfindsamer* style to a truly expressive musical language. His keyboard compositions which have been preserved include twelve fugues and six polonaises,[31] but these masterworks have fallen into an entirely undeserved oblivion. His polonaises, one example of which is shown in Figure 82, are wonderful examples of idealized dance music, comparable to Orlando Gibbons' "Pavane" or to the allemandes, courantes, sarabandes, and gigues in the suites of Johann Sebastian Bach. In their bold expressiveness and dynamic intensity they come suprisingly close to the musical language of Beethoven.

It is a much-discussed, though somewhat idle, question, whether

82. W. F. BACH—*Polonaise*

·179·

Wilhelm Friedemann Bach or his brother Karl Philipp Emanuel was the greater artist. There is reason to think that Wilhelm Friedemann was the more outstanding talent, but it is certainly true that Karl Philipp achieved more important results from the point of view of historic progress. To call him, as is frequently done, "the inventor of the modern sonata," is, of course, an unadmissible simplification of a very complex phenomenon. He is one among the many composers, German as well as Italian, who worked toward the same goal, and it is only his greater seriousness of purpose and his deeper insight into the problems which make him stand out as the most important predecessor of the Viennese classics. His influence is more clearly apparent in the works of Haydn and Beethoven than in those of Mozart, as his musical style lacks the natural simplicity and charm which we so greatly admire in Mozart. Karl Philipp tends toward exaggeration of expression, an exaggeration which is not wholly the result of creative abundance, but also of intellectual reflection with the resulting tendency to overstate the case. Nevertheless, one cannot help admiring the courage with which he holds his position, the typical position of one who sees possibilities without being able to realize them. This may be called imperfection—but it is the imperfection of one whose ideas are ahead of his technical means, not of one whose technical skill is ahead of his ideas, as is the case with so many modern composers.

K. P. E. Bach wrote a considerable number of sonatas during the period from 1742 to 1787. It should be remembered that this is the time during which the pianoforte rose to prominence over the harpsichord and the clavichord; this change is clearly reflected in these sonatas. The earliest sonatas are all written for the clavichord, which was his favorite instrument. Of his six sets *für Kenner und Liebhaber* (for Connoisseurs and Amateurs), as they are named, the first, published in 1779, is still called "Claviersonaten," probably indicating an ad-libitum use of the clavichord, harpsichord, or pianoforte, while the other five, published from 1780 to 1787, expressly call for the "Forte-piano."

83. K. P. E. BACH—*Andante from a Sonata*

·182·

Karl Philipp Emanuel Bach attained the most perfect realization of his intentions in his slow movements. The slow movement of his first sonata (Fig. 83) ,* written in 1742, is a composition which ranks high above the mediocrities produced by the Rococo composers of the period. The alternation of an expressive melody and an affecting recitative exhibits a poetic vision which anticipates Schumann by almost one hundred years.

* According to the stylistic principles of the recitative the first of two double notes such as at the beginning of measure 1 of system II is to be replaced by its upper neighbor note (appogiatura). Therefore, the initial notes of measures 1, 2, 3 of system II should be played respectively as b-flat, d-sharp, and c-sharp. Similarly later on. In measure 3 of system IV play g g d instead of g d d.

1770 — CLASSICISM — 1830

KARL PHILIPP EMANUEL BACH's immediate successor was Josef
Haydn (1732–1809), the first master of musical classicism,[32] that great
period which has aptly been described as a synthesis of "nature and
humanity." In order to understand Haydn's position in music history
it must be realized that he lived almost eighty years and that, like
few other composers (Verdi was one), his creative imagination grew
steadily from decade to decade, reaching its culmination in his latest
works. Only these latest works, the last symphonies, quartets, and
oratorios, are commonly performed today. Numerous compositions,
particularly those of his middle period, are hardly known even to musical scholars, except the few specialists who have devoted themselves to
the study of his works. His thirty-five sonatas for the pianoforte all
belong to his early or middle period (1760–1780). Artistically
they cannot quite compare with the maturity of his latest symphonies
and quartets. Nevertheless, a study of these little-known sonatas shows
that little justice is done to Haydn if he is judged only by his latest
works. His early sonatas clearly reveal not only the influence of Karl
Philipp Emanuel Bach, but also that decisive change from studied
expressiveness to natural expression which inaugurated a new era of
musical language. Moreover, for the final movements of his sonatas
Haydn frequently used an entirely novel style of joyous vitality,
sprightly humor, and sparkling wit which no other master has expressed more fortunately. The first and last movement of a sonata in
E-major, written in 1767, are given here as an illustration (Fig. 84).

These movements also serve as our first examples of that important and interesting musical form which, from Haydn and his predecessors to Brahms and Bruckner, has been used time and again in sonatas, string quartets, symphonies, and so on, and which is known under the somewhat misleading name of sonata-form. Misleading, because this term does not indicate the form of the sonata (as consisting of three or four movements, for example allegro, adagio, scherzo, allegro), but the special form used almost invariably for the first movement and frequently for other movements also. Without entering into a detailed description of this form, it will suffice to say that a movement written in sonata-form falls into three sections, known as exposition (E), development (D), and recapitulation (R). In the exposition the composer introduces his musical ideas, consisting of a number, from two to five or more, of distinct and frequently contrasting themes (I, II, etc.) which are connected by transitional passages. In the development some of these themes, or short motives derived thereof, are "developed," that is, treated in a manner similar to the process which leads from a small cell to a full-grown organism. The recapitulation repeats the exposition, though with certain modifications of the harmonic theme which are relatively unimportant from the listener's point of view.

Sonata-form is frequently described as an example of ternary form, a term which is used in music for compositions showing the pattern A B A. Although at first glance this interpretation would seem to be in agreement with the above description of sonata-form, it nevertheless is inaccurate and misleading, mainly because it overlooks (or dismisses) the signs of repeat which are found in nearly all the examples of sonata-form written between 1750 and 1870. In our two movements by Haydn such signs of repeat are found at the end of the exposition as well as of the recapitulation. Such a structure suggests a binary rather than a ternary scheme. It can indeed be shown that sonata-form developed from pieces written in binary form, such as the dance movements in the suites of Bach. In fact, these movements very neatly illustrate the earliest stages of this most interesting process of

84. HAYDN—*Sonata*

Finale.
Presto.

evolution. The allemande from Bach's French Suite No. VI, reproduced on p. 147, represents that simplest type of binary form which may be termed "symmetrical," owing to the equal (or nearly equal) length of its first and second sections. The other movements illustrate a more "developed" type of binary form, of asymmetrical construction, in which the second section is longer than the first, frequently twice as long. This procedure clearly indicates the tendency towards "development" which forms an essential feature of sonata-form. Among these asymmetrical pieces the minuet most clearly indicates a third step of evolution, characterized by the restatement of the first section (or, at least, its initial theme) at the end of the second section, a method which clearly foreshadows the recapitulation of sonata-form. There still remained one important step to be taken, that is, the change from the continuous and strictly monothematic style of the dance movements to a contrast style leading to an extended exposition with two or, later on, three and more, different themes. As early as 1720 we find fully-developed examples of sonata-form in the chamber music works by Francesco Maria Veracini (an exact contemporary of Bach, 1685–1750), and K. P. E. Bach consistently used this form for the fast movements of his piano sonatas.

All these examples of sonata-form, as well as those found in the sonatas and early symphonies by Haydn and Mozart, show the double repeats, one for the exposition, the other for the development plus recapitulation, which more than anything clearly point to the binary form as the root of sonata-form. In their late symphonies, however, these two masters usually employed a simplified scheme in which the exposition is still repeated, while the repeat of the second, much longer, section is abandoned. Thus was established the classical type of sonata-form as we find it in the sonatas, symphonies, and chamber music of Beethoven, Schubert, and others. No doubt, this step toward simplification was eminently justified and, indeed, might well have been taken at a somewhat earlier time. The repetition of the second section, as found in the earlier works of Haydn and Mozart, can hardly be considered other than a historical formalism without aesthetic justification, since the very nature of the development section seems to militate against its being played twice. The repeat of the exposition, however, is an altogether different matter which should not be treated in the light and thoughtless manner of most of our present-day conductors and pianists, who habitually omit this repeat in their performances. This habit, although perhaps justifiable in certain special cases, is on the whole to be deplored. There can be no doubt that Haydn, Mozart, and their successors wanted the exposition to be played twice, the more so since they frequently took the trouble of writing two different endings for it, the first of which leads back to the beginning, while the second leads on to the development. No doubt, the composers were fully aware of the aesthetic significance of this repetition, which greatly contributes to impress on the hearer's mind the themes on which the whole movement is based, and which also causes the beginning of the development section to appear in its proper light—as a decisive step in a new direction.[33]

At the time when Haydn wrote the sonata which served as the point of departure for the foregoing discussion, Wolfgang Amadeus Mozart (1756–1791) was a boy of ten, but one who had already startled the world as a child prodigy. No greater contrast of musical careers can be imagined than that of Mozart's and Haydn's. It is the contrast between a life which came to its natural end at a biblical number of years, and one which was abruptly terminated when it had just begun to unfold. It is the contrast between a slow and patient process of maturing, and a brilliant outburst of artistic greatness the like of which has hardly ever been seen in the world of music. Different though Haydn and Mozart were in age and temperament, they nevertheless present a unique example of collaboration and mutual completion, of an exchange of ideas in which the younger man gave just as much to the older as he took.

Mozart's compositions for the pianoforte are mostly sonatas and variations. While Haydn, in his piano sonatas, built chiefly upon the work of Karl Philipp Emanuel Bach, Mozart was indebted to yet another Bach, Johann Sebastian's youngest son Johann Christian Bach

(1735–1782), who is known as the Milanese or the London Bach because he spent his life outside of Germany in these places. Johann Christian's stay in Italy brought him into contact with the Italian Rococo style of Rutini, Pescetti, and Grazioli, to whose superficial suavity he brought a healthy admixture of German directness and seriousness. The combination of these elements resulted in a style which is surprisingly close to that of the young Mozart, as the beginning of his piano sonata in B-flat (Fig. 85) shows. Mozartian though this music may sound, we clearly feel, of course, the distance which separates it from the real Mozart. A difference like this is easily felt, though much less easily described and explained. As in the case of Johann Sebastian Bach and his predecessor Fischer, whom we con-

85.

sidered in Chapter 5, the artistic superiority of Mozart over Johann Christian Bach is, in the first place, a superiority of melodic inspiration. There is a pianoforte sonata by Mozart, also in B-flat, the first theme of which bears a certain resemblance to that of Bach's sonata and which therefore lends itself rather well to the purpose of comparison (Fig. 86).

The principles of melodic analysis explained and employed in Chapter 5 will prove helpful here too. If we look at these two melodies

86.

from the point of view of their linear design, and if we try to interpret this design as the tangible result of musical forces, the basic difference between them will readily appear. No doubt, Bach's theme, in spite of its seeming liveliness, does not achieve much. It moves somewhat aimlessly around its axis, repeating itself and falling back, after a few measures, to exactly the same point where it started. Mozart's theme, on the other hand, with its interplay of rising and falling tendencies, closely interlocked and mutually conditioned, shows true animation, resilience, and balance.

Mozart wrote eighteen piano sonatas. Most of these were written between 1774 and 1778, when he was eighteen to twenty-two. The first movement, reproduced here (Fig. 87), of a sonata in C-major written in 1777 shows him in full command of the stylistic and formal elements involved in sonata writing. The exposition clearly falls into neatly contrasting sections (marked below I and II), in each of which a number of distinct themes can be distinguished (marked 1, 2, etc.). Particularly interesting is the development section, for it reveals an admirable grasp and command of that "motival" technique which

87. MOZART—*Sonata*

·195·

88. MOZART—*Air Varié*

represents the final step in the evolution of the classical sonata-form. The term "motival" indicates that the piece or the section in question is based, not on full-length melodies or phrases, but on brief, though self-contained, fragments thereof. A glance at the development sections of the two movements by Haydn will illustrate the difference between the earlier method in which full phrases prevail, and the novel technique of motive, which became established in the late works of Haydn and Mozart, and was brought to the highest perfection by Beethoven and Brahms. Mozart's development section is based mainly on the initial motive of the first theme. This is indicated in our illustration by the letter m.

No less important and beautiful than his sonatas, though much less known, are Mozart's variations for pianoforte. Although variations are one of the oldest forms of keyboard music and a form which was extremely frequent in the literature of the seventeenth century, it was rather little cultivated during the eighteenth century, until Mozart raised it to new artistic significance. Aside from various movements in his sonatas which are written in this form, Mozart wrote about twenty independent compositions of this type. Among these is one which he composed at the age of nine years and which, in spite of its childlike simplicity, not only possesses an undeniable charm but also shows an amazing command of the technique of composition. Figure 88 shows the theme together with two of the eight variations.

Some twenty years later he wrote variations on a French tune, "La belle Française" (Fig. 89) which are among his most mature and most beautiful compositions. While in the early composition each variation is nothing more than the theme lightly disguised, those of "La belle Française" bear the stamp of full individuality. Naturally,

89. MOZART—*Variations, La belle Française*

VAR. II.

VAR. IV.

VAR. IX.
Minore.

VAR. XI.
Adagio.

poco   a   poco   cre - scen - do

these variations also are disguises—as in a way all variations are—but what in the early pieces was childlike play, has now become an art of high refinement and perfection. The early variations all belong to the simplest type of variation in which the melody as well as the harmonies of the theme is retained, the former being somewhat modified by the application of a fixed pattern of ornamentation. Some variations of the late set belong to the same category, for instance, the first or the second. Others, however, represent a more advanced and more interesting type of variation, in which only the harmonies of the theme are retained while the original tune is replaced by a new melody, as in the fourth, the seventh, or the ninth variation, the last of which also introduces the change from the major into the minor key.

Finally, it may be observed that in practically all the variations by Mozart the last but one is in slow tempo, adagio, while the last is in fast tempo, allegro or presto, and also in a different meter, for example, triple meter if the theme is in duple meter, or duple meter if the theme is in triple, as is the case here.

We now turn to a consideration of the piano works of Beethoven. The name of Ludwig van Beethoven (1770–1827) stands out as the very symbol of greatness in music. Only one other composer has a stature comparable or equal to his; this is Bach, who excels as the great master of the fugue as Beethoven excels in the field of the sonata. Considering certain present-day trends it is perhaps advisable to reverse the order of the names in this sentence, and to state that Beethoven's stature is comparable or equal to that of Bach. There is a tendency among a considerable group of serious musicians to elevate Bach to an even higher rank than Beethoven, and in certain circles it has become a sort of fashion to dismiss Beethoven as a composer of lesser significance. It is certainly true that too much praise can never be given Bach, whose every work is a miracle of art, but to do so at the expense of Beethoven indicates a narrowness of mind no less than that of former generations to whom Bach was dull and all but incomprehensible. One of the leaders in the modern "Back to Bach" movement and one of the first who dared to criticize certain traits of Beethoven's style was the German writer and composer August Halm. I had the good fortune to come in close contact with this man whose writings on music are by far the most profound I have yet encountered. I remember a conversation I had with him some twenty years ago in which the question came up what a modern Noah should do if, preparing for another flood, he were permitted to take into his ark just one music book to be preserved for future generations. Halm's answer, after a short deliberation, was, "Beethoven's sonatas." "Why not," I exclaimed, "Bach's *Well-tempered Clavier?*" knowing how highly he valued it. "Because the *Well-tempered Clavier* is one book, and Beethoven's sonatas are thirty-two books." This is, it seems to me, a very true observation and one which reveals one of the most fundamental facts about Beethoven. Bach's preludes and fugues, each an outstanding masterwork of musical art, are nevertheless examples of a type, as are, even more so, the sonatas, quartets, and symphonies of Mozart and Haydn. Beethoven, with characteristic daring, approached this problem from an entirely new point of view, making each composition an individual in its own right, essentially different from any other one. It is hardly necessary to point out that his procedure became the precedent for all composers after him,[34] so much so that their tendency to make each composition something different frequently took on the form of a forced striving for novelty at any price. The question may well be raised whether, from a long-range point of view, the new approach to musical composition was as clearly a change for the better as the modern observer is naturally inclined to think at first. But there can be no doubt that, in the case of Beethoven and of others after him, it has produced truly magnificent results.

It should be noticed that there are actually more than thirty-two Beethoven sonatas, and that none of the current editions is complete. True enough, the missing four or six sonatas [35] are works of his early youth, composed in Bonn (*c.* 1780) before he came to Vienna, and written in close imitation of Haydn and Mozart. Nevertheless, they are not lacking in certain interesting features, and at any rate they

Larghetto maestoso.

Allegro assai.

·209·

91. BEETHOVEN—*Sonata*—OP. 2, NO. 1

should be known if only in order to illustrate the background and starting point of a great master. Particularly remarkable is a sonata in F-minor (the first movement of which is reproduced in Figure 90) which Beethoven composed in 1781, at the age of eleven years. The very choice of a key which is hardly, if ever, encountered in the sonatas and symphonies of Haydn and Mozart, indicates a daring, characteristic of the man throughout his life. The expression seems to foreshadow the composer of the C-minor symphony and the "Appassionata." The slow introduction, which recurs before the recapitulation, calls to mind a similar method used in the "Sonata Pathéthique." Striking though this early sonata is, there is, of course, a wide separation between its youthful boldness and the mature strength of what is usually considered his first sonata, op. 2, no. 1, also in F-minor, which he wrote in Vienna at the age of twenty-five. Figure 91 shows the exposition of the first movement of this sonata.

In order to obtain a correct picture of the chronological development of Beethoven's sonatas it should be observed that some sonatas which, owing to their opus numbers, figure as relatively late works, actually are of a much earlier date, the opus number indicating only the time of their publication, not of their composition. To this group belong the two sonatas opus 49, the second of which is well known to every young piano student (Fig. 92).

92.

The proper chronological place for this sonata would probably be between the early sonata of 1781 and the opus 2 of 1795. Disregarding these preliminary works, it is interesting to notice that all the sonatas were composed in the decade between 1795 and 1805, except for the last eight, which followed in wide intervals between 1808 and 1822. Thus, Beethoven's sonatas fall clearly into three groups: the eight early sonatas written between about 1780 and 1790; the twenty-two sonatas of the middle period, written between 1795 and 1805; and the eight late sonatas from 1808 to 1822. Those of the middle period are by far the best known. They comprise such famous works as the "Pathétique," the "Moonlight Sonata," the "Waldstein Sonata," and the "Appassionata" which is the last of this group.

It was particularly in the works of his middle period that Beethoven arrived at that style and that musical expression which forever have become associated with his name. Different generations have given different interpretations of this style and expression. During his lifetime he was mostly admired for his freedom of inspiration, for his boldness of spirit, for his unbridled flight of fancy. Indeed, to the people who had grown up with K. P. E. Bach, Haydn, and Mozart, Beethoven was bound to appear as the great liberator, the revolutionary hero. Later, when his innovations had become accepted as the foundation stone of a new era of musical thought, he was celebrated as one of the great leaders of mankind, side by side with Plato, Michelangelo, Shakespeare, and Goethe. His works were felt to be symbols, not so much of heroic daring, but of the eternal ideals of humanity. Today we are inclined to think that such interpretations, though not wholly without significance, do not reveal the full truth about Beethoven, and that his real greatness lies in the purely musical quality of his work. A supreme mastery in handling the problems of musical form and style, a unique power of elaboration and climactic development, an incomparable dynamic quality, an admirable conciseness of language, an inevitable logic of thought—these are some of the most outstanding traits of his musical personality. August Halm, whose pertinent dictum about Bach and Beethoven has been previously mentioned, has happily summarized these traits by saying that Beethoven is the great strategic genius of music. As a matter of fact, Beethoven's approach to, and treatment of, music is not unlike that of a commander using his forces with the greatest skill, always at the right moment and at the right place. In this respect he represents the strongest possible contrast to Bach. For Bach, music is a divine substance—for Beethoven, a creation of man; where Bach serves in pious devotion, Beethoven rules in supreme sovereignty.

Turning to a more technical consideration of Beethoven's sonatas, a study of his themes proves most engrossing and illuminating. The first theme of the first piano sonata, in F-minor, may serve as a point of departure (Fig. 93). What shall we say about this melody? What meaning is attached to it, what message does it convey? Is it beautiful? Perhaps, though hardly in the ordinary sense of the word. Is it expressive, emotional? Yes, but so are thousands of others. Is it forceful, or stormy, or passionate? Possibly, but so are hundreds of others. Obviously, these designations are too general to serve for anything but a very broad and, therefore, rather meaningless characterization. A more penetrating analysis is necessary in order to understand the individual character of this melody, as distinguished from others which are no less expressive, forceful, or passionate, and it is only on

93.

the basis of such individual analyses that we may be able to arrive at valid and meaningful conclusions of a more general nature. Various attempts have been made to establish useful methods of melodic analysis, some of which involve rather farfetched and debatable principles. Little attention, however, has been paid to what is, no doubt, the most natural approach to this problem, that is, a consideration based on the fact that any melody consists of a succession of tones varying in pitch, and therefore moving up and down in a manner reminiscent of a geometrical curve. The principles of this method have been briefly expounded in the section on Bach. Beethoven's compositions offer no less convincing examples for it than do those of Bach, although of a totally different character, as a study of the theme from the first piano sonata readily shows. This theme opens with a boldly ascending motion in large steps through the tones of the f-minor triad, reaching immediately a first high point on the tone a-flat from which it falls back, as if under the reaction of elasticity. There follows another motion of the same design (measures 3 to 4) but leading to a higher peak, the tone b-flat. Not satisfied with the energy contained in these two lines, Beethoven repeats each of them in a characteristically shortened form, reduced to its crest formation (measures 5 to 6). As the result of these redoubled and repeated attacks the culmination of the whole melody is reached in the tone c of measure 7, and this is followed by a descending motion in which the accumulated energies are released.

This is only one of the many examples to be found in Beethoven's works which demonstrate, in a fascinating variety of designs, that dynamic vitality which is the basic trait of Beethoven's musical language. It is quite significant that nearly all the themes found in Beethoven's compositions, particularly those of the middle period, show a clearly ascending design or, more properly, a design in which the ascending energy prevails over the descending tendencies, the latter appearing only in order to put the former into relief. One more example may be given in order to illustrate this important point: the first theme of the pianoforte sonata in D-major, op. 10, no. 3 (Fig. 94).

94.

This theme opens with a short descending line of four notes which, however, serve only to reach the starting point for a long ascending line, leading to a first point of repose, on the high a (measure 4). From here the melody descends relaxedly, through the initial motive of four descending notes (measures 5 to 10); this motive, by the way, plays a prominent part throughout the whole movement. In the following measures (11 to 16) the preceding phrase is restated in a forceful variation which closes with a convincing expression of finality. Actually, however, the musical forces do not stop here. There follows (measures 17 to 22) a third ascending motion similar to that of the beginning but leading to a much higher point, the final culmination of all the previous energies.

No less interesting than a study of Beethoven's themes is a study of how they are used during the course of the movement, particularly in the development section. It was inevitable that Beethoven, the unrivaled master of musical strategy, should give the greatest attention to this section, much more so than did Haydn and Mozart, who only in some of their latest symphonies approximated what Beethoven achieved. In Beethoven's development sections the technical devices of modulation, fragmentation, reiteration, combination, and so on, are vested with a new significance. They are used in such a way as to bring about a feeling of evolution and growth, of increased intensity and higher temperature, of dynamic stress and climax, of a battlefield where the musical forces come to grips. Particularly frequent and effective is a technique which, for the purpose of short reference, may be called segmentation. This means that a theme, instead of being presented in full, is cut into halves, and that only the second half is used for the continuation. It will be remembered that we encountered an example of this technique in our consideration of the theme from the first pianoforte sonata, in which the initial ascending line was reduced to the short crest motive which forms the close. The development sections of Beethoven's sonatas, symphonies, and so on show numerous examples of the same technique, applied even more deliberately and profusely. Particularly interesting in this respect is the first movement of the sonata in D-major, op. 28. The first theme of this movement—by the way, one of the few themes of Beethoven in which descending motion prevails—is shown in Figure 95.

95.

At the beginning of the development section (Fig. 96) this theme appears twice in its full shape, first in major, then in minor. After this there starts an extended process of successive segmentation in which the theme is reduced to its second half, which is played several times in alternation between the right and the left hand. Starting with measure 6 of system IV the four-measure motive is reduced to one of two measures, and this is used again in alternation of high and low. Finally this is cut down to a one-measure motive which is repeated over and over again, like incessant strokes of a hammer.

We must be content with these sketchy remarks and examples as an illustration of Beethoven's middle period. His late sonatas, particularly the last six written between 1814 and 1822, reveal a composer far different from the one who wrote the "Moonlight Sonata," the

96. BEETHOVEN—*Sonata*—OP. 28

"Pathétique," the "Appassionata," the Fifth Symphony, or the "Emperor Concerto." At the very summit of a mastery for which there are few parallels in the history of music, Beethoven, as if unsatisfied with this achievement, embarked on a new road towards distant and unexplored regions. It was a hazardous and uncertain road, leading from manifest results of the highest order to new questions and problems, from the idealized corporeality of his mature style to a metaphysical and visionary transcendentalism, from the attitude of a sovereign commander to that of a searcher for new truths. It brought about works which stand in the same relationship to the "Waldstein Sonata" and the "Emperor Concerto" as does Shakespeare's *Tempest* to his *Romeo and Juliet,* or Goethe's *Faust* to his *Tasso,* or Rembrandt's "Christ at Emmaus" to his "Anatomy Lesson."

It is interesting to notice that Beethoven's late style is much more clearly indicated in his piano sonatas and string quartets than in his symphonies, the three last of which belong chronologically to his late period. Probably the explanation is found in the fact that the orchestra, with its large and varied resources, compelled him to retain that attitude of an organizer and strategist which he abandoned in

·219·

his works for the pianoforte and the string quartet. What are the main characteristics of Beethoven's late compositions? First, a freer treatment of the formal structure of the sonata. Of the eight sonatas written after the "Appassionata," not one follows the standard form of the sonata. Some of them have only two movements; in others the traditional scheme is somewhat enlarged by the insertion of short transitional movements. Frequently the final movement is a fugue, or the first movement shows a character of sublimated lyricism quite different from its customary expression of dynamic tension. In matters of style it is extremely difficult to make valid statements of a general nature, although the complete novelty of this style is immediately apparent to the listener. The distinctive qualities of the late Beethoven can hardly be grasped by analytical methods, they can only be absorbed through the reception of the work as an indivisible whole. Only one of the most obvious and characteristic traits can be mentioned here: the use of extremely wide spacing for simultaneous tones. There are many passages in the late sonatas where the right hand plays just one or two tones near the upper end of the keyboard, while the left hand adds a bass note in the lower register, at a distance of five or more octáves. One of these, from the slow movement of op. 110,

97.

is reproduced here (Fig. 97, a). It is interesting to compare the effect of this passage with that of Figure 97, b, which shows the same passage in the conventional style of writing.

Many musicians and writers on music have considered this and other features of the last sonatas as "bad piano style," and, with forgiving condescension, have explained it either as the result of Beethoven's deafness, or as the fanciful whim of the man who once made a remark about "that contemptible violin." Such explanations do not deserve to be taken seriously. They are indicative of a confusion, frequently encountered in discussions and writings on music, between the auditory senses and the musical ear. The former are a category of the purely perceptive faculties—the latter, of the mental powers. Quite possibly, the auditory senses find little satisfaction in the sound of this passage. It does not matter whether they do or not. The musical ear, however, cannot fail to be immensely satisfied by the two widely separated lines moving in opposite directions and creating a tension which would be completely destroyed if they were brought more closely together, or if the empty space between them were filled in by massive sounds. They represent an artistic phenomenon comparable to ancient Chinese drawings in which two widely separated brush strokes create an artistic reality of far greater significance than any amount of oil color could ever produce.

The exposition of the first movement of Beethoven's sonata in A-flat major, op. 110, is given here (Fig. 98) as an example of his late piano style. It has that quality of transcendent lyricism which steps forth so frequently in the late sonatas and string quartets.

During the thirty years which Beethoven spent in Vienna there lived, not far from him in the same city, a great composer whom he never met, who was his junior by almost thirty years, but who died only one year after him: Franz Schubert (1797–1828). Schubert is usually considered a Romantic composer, side by side with Robert Schumann—with whom he is frequently confused—Mendelssohn, and Chopin. Such a classification is somewhat misleading. Schubert's music does, no doubt, indicate the trend towards Romanticism; on the other hand, it is firmly rooted in the classical tradition, and the classical tradition is preponderant. Schubert's symphonies, quartets, piano trios, and his piano sonatas in particular show him to be the immediate heir to the tradition of Beethoven, and even his songs, in which the Romantic element naturally emerges more clearly, show the classical traits of melody, harmony, and form. Naturally, such considerations are largely a matter of personal interpretation.

BEETHOVEN—*Sonata*—OP. 110

Moderato cantabile, molto espressivo.

By and large, however, an understanding of Schubert's music is facilitated if, instead of being grouped together with Mendelssohn, Schumann, Chopin, and Liszt (all of whom were his juniors by more than ten years), he is given a place at the end of the classical school and leading into the Romantic movement.

Although Schubert's fame rests mainly upon his songs, those immortal masterworks which have never been equaled by any other composers, his compositions for the piano are hardly less important and beautiful, although much less known. His sonatas especially are, to the present day, misunderstood and neglected. For instance, the following sentences are found in a reference book which appeared some years ago: "Schubert's piano sonatas . . . exhibit side by side some of his strongest and his weakest qualities. Their themes are repeatedly too melodically beautiful, too long-breathed, too complete and song-like in themselves for purposes of any development that is more than a process of repetition in different keys or a play of arabesque and ornamentation. The discrepancies between the musical character and the emotional significance and weight of various movements are often such as to impair the deeper unity of the work." Aside from the fact that these remarks betray, on the whole, a depreciating attitude which is not justified, they contain a mixture of true and false statements which are far from giving an adequate picture. It is true that Schubert's themes are melodically beautiful, long-breathed, and songlike, but they are hardly more so than the themes in some of Beethoven's sonatas, for example, that of the first movement from the sonata op. 110. More pertinent is the remark regarding the development of Schubert's themes. His development technique differs indeed from that of Beethoven, for he employs repetition of entire melodies rather than the "motival" devices of segmentation, fragmentation, combination, and so on, characteristic of Beethoven. Nevertheless, he uses this different technique with such an admirable ingenuity and with such marvelous results that it must be considered as a' new procedure with its own standing, all the more since it was taken over and brought to a wonderful culmination in the symphonies of Anton

Bruckner, who resembles Schubert in many respects. As regards the relationship between the various movements of Schubert's sonatas, the discrepancy between their musical character and emotional significance is no less and no more than in any sonata by Beethoven. It is true, however, that in a number of Schubert's sonatas the various movements are of uneven artistic quality so that, for instance, first and second movements of great beauty are combined with a last movement of a somewhat inferior rank. At least three of his piano sonatas, however, are masterworks from the first to the last note, which really means something since the distance between these two notes is rather long indeed; it is by no means too long, however, if the length of a musical composition is judged, not by the minutes it takes to perform, but by the artistic quality and significance of its contents.

The most outstanding of Schubert's piano sonatas is the one in B-flat major, composed in 1828, shortly before he died. Its second movement, which is reproduced here (Fig. 99), represents one of the most extraordinarily beautiful peregrinations in all music. It is, one might feel, the swan song announcing the end, not only of a great man, but also of a great period—the period which achieved the most perfect balance of expression and form, of humanity and nature, of the mind and the world.

99. SCHUBERT—*Sonata*

·229·

1830 — ROMANTICISM — 1900

THE SUBJECT OF THIS CHAPTER is the pianoforte music of the Romantic movement. It is the music of Schumann, Mendelssohn, Chopin, Liszt, and Brahms—music which more than any other is dear to the hearts of music lovers and to the hands of pianists. It is music more captivating, more emotional, more exciting, and more soothing than any music written before or after. It is Romantic music in the truest sense of the word.

The Romantic movement in Germany originated in a literary school of the late eighteenth century, formed by writers such as Novalis (1772–1801) and Tieck (1773–1853) who, in search for relief from the supposed or real prosiness and shallowness of their surroundings, went back to the literature and culture of the Middle Ages, with its valiant knights, gracious ladies, and pious monks. Shortly after 1800 musicians came under the influence of this literary movement. For them it meant, not a return to the music of the Middle Ages (which at that time was entirely unknown and, at any rate, would certainly not have been a source of inspiration for them), but a general attitude of "longing for something nonexistent," a propensity for dream and fancy, for unrestrained subjectivism and emotionalism. In fact, music soon proved to be a much more fertile ground for the novel tendencies than literature or any other art, owing, no doubt, to the intangible character of its material, sound. Romantic writers like E. T. A. Hoffmann and Stendhal extolled music as "the Romantic art," or said that "music is always Romantic."

Romantic music is the immediate expression of the human soul, with all its emotions of joy and sorrow, of passion and tenderness, of exuberance and despair. More specifically, it is the expression of those feelings which cannot be satisfied, or which want to remain unsated even though they could be satisfied. It is this state of mind which distinguishes the Romantic composer from, for instance, Beethoven, whose compositions are, in a way, no less emotional than those of the Romanticists. For Beethoven, however, emotion is something which can be fully translated into a musical idiom, and all his efforts are directed towards the realization of this objective. The Romantic composer, on the other hand, feels that such a realization can never be attained. He is always in search of the "blue flower," the mystic symbol of his longing and dreaming.

The Romantic mind is frequently described as one that divorces what theretofore had been inseparable aspects of a unified conception: the inner and the outer world, or dream and reality. More to the point, perhaps, is the almost opposite interpretation: the Romanticist includes reality in his dream world, instead of facing it as an objective phenomenon. Thus the line of demarcation between outside and inside is effaced, a mental process which falls in line with other basic traits of Romanticism, all of which betray a tendency towards the blurring of borderlines. One of these traits is the close amalgamation of music with the other arts, particularly literature. Composers not only take a strong interest in literature and frequently maintain personal ties with outstanding writers, they also think of themselves as "tone-poets," as men who express poetry in the much subtler language of sounds; they write pieces with literary titles such as "Novelette," "Ballade," and "Album Leaf," or they compose "symphonic poems," translating into music literary subjects such as Hamlet, Romeo and Juliet, or Till Eulenspiegel.

This integration of the outer world with the inner self, this "subjective universalism," as it has been called,[36] also brought about that interesting phenomenon of dual personality which steps forth so clearly in the Romantic composer par excellence, Robert Schumann

(1810–1856) . Schumann liked to think of himself as being two characters, one contemplative and dreamy, the other impetuous and realistic—or, to use terms of present-day psychology, one introvert and the other extrovert. He went so far as to give these characters the appearance of reality, calling the former Eusebius, the latter Florestan, names under which they appear in his numerous writings on music, as members of that imaginary circle which he called the *Davidsbund* (the David-League) , and to which he entrusted the fight against the musical Philistines, the mediocre drawing-room composers of his day. It was natural for Schumann to make this literary idea a musical reality as well, and so he did in one of his earliest works, op. 6, the *Davidsbündlertänze* (Dances of the David-Leaguers) , a collection of most charming pieces, each of which is signed either "E," for Eusebius, or "F," for Florestan. Some of the eighteen pieces in this collection are reproduced here (Fig. 100) .

Friedrich Gundolf, former professor of German literature at the University of Heidelberg, once made the remark that Romanticism "began as gun powder, continued as magic powder, and ended as sleeping powder." Although this remark was made in reference to literary Romanticism, for which it is especially significant, it also characterizes certain traits of the musical movement. It is particularly applicable to Schumann himself, whose creative career started, continued, and ended in just such a manner. Compared with the soaring spirit and the lively imagination of his early works, those of the thirty-five-year-old are largely routine products of a mind thriving on the riches of the past, while those of the forty-year-old are tragic tokens of artistic impotence, foreshadowing the mental collapse which preceded his early death. Some isolated exceptions notwithstanding, Schumann's most outstanding and original compositions fall within the opus numbers from 1 to 21, written between 1830 and 1838. All these works are for the pianoforte, and nearly all of them belong to that typically Romantic category of piano music which may be designated as "Character piece." This is a short piece of a unified design and expression, clearly suggestive of a definite mood or a programmatic idea which, in fact, is frequently indicated in titles such as "In the Evening," "Dream Visions," "Entreating Child," or "The Poet Speaks." Schumann frequently combined, under a collective title, a number, ten or twenty, of such short pieces to be played in succession, similar to the songs of a song cycle. There resulted a typically Romantic form which, in spite of its considerable extension, was extremely flexible, and not subject to any formal principles such as enter

100. SCHUMANN—*Davidsbündlertänze*—OP. 6

Einfach. (M.M. ♩= 96.)

Nº 5.

Zart und singend.(M.M. ♩ = 100.)

N.º 14.

Coda.

·237·

into the sonata. To this category belong the *Dances of the David-Leaguers* as well as his *Papillons, Scenes from Childhood,* and *Carnaval*—each a fanciful story told in a succession of little scenes. It is interesting to notice that the creator of this form was Beethoven, whose two sets of *Bagatellen,* op. 119 and op. 126, are collections of short character pieces of exactly this type, which probably served Schumann as a model. Even more numerous than these "character cycles," as one may call them, are single pieces similar in purpose to those which occur in the cycles, though naturally more extended, usually in the scheme of the three-part form, A B A, that is, with a contrasting middle section B, after which the first section is repeated. Schubert's Impromptus and Moments musicaux are among the earliest examples of this type. Numerous composers of the Romantic period have written such character pieces, and it will suffice to mention, in addition to Schubert, Schumann with his Intermezzi and Novellettes, Mendelssohn with his Songs Without Words, Chopin's Preludes, Nocturnes, and Etudes, Brahms' Ballades, Rhapsodies, Fantasies, and Capriccios, Grieg's Lyrical Pieces, and Debussy's Images and Preludes, in order to indicate the scope of this repertory.

It is easy to understand why the character piece found such favor with the Romantic composers. It is an extremely simple form and one which leaves the composer entirely free as to contents, enabling him to use it as the vehicle of expression for every conceivable mood, emotion, or vision. On the other hand, the sonata which Beethoven had raised to the highest point of artistic significance declined under their hands to a mere shadow of its former self. The essentially dynamic and masculine character of the sonata did not agree with the somewhat effeminate lyricism of composers like Schumann, Mendelssohn, and Chopin. Schumann's three piano sonatas are a pathetic effort to simulate strength, substituting, as they do, self-intoxication for vitality. This self-intoxication is particularly patent in his habit of repeating ad nauseam a simple rhythm or motive, chasing it aimlessly through pages and pages of the score. For instance, in his Grande Sonata, op. 11, one idea occupies more than half of the first movement (Fig. 101).

High above Schumann's sonatas proper stands his Fantasia in C-major, op. 17, a *sonata quasi una fantasia* (to borrow a pertinent designation from Beethoven's op. 27, no. 1, universally known as the

101.

"Moonlight Sonata") in three movements, the first and last of which
are truly remarkable for their imaginative flight of fancy, while the
middle movement suffers somewhat from the monotony of self-repe-
tition. The beginning of the last movement is given in Figure 102.

Schumann was born in 1810, and at approximately the same time
three other Romantic composers were born: Chopin, Mendelssohn,
and Liszt. Frédéric François Chopin (1810–1849), of half French and
half Polish extraction, was, on the whole, a more vigorous musical personality than Schumann, more susceptible to visions of grandeur and
burning passion. Although a Romanticist in the truest sense of the
word, he succeeded, in two of his piano sonatas, the B-flat minor and
the B-minor, in recreating this classical form as an exciting drama,

Langsam getragen. Durchweg leise zu halten. M.M. ♩.= 66.

·242·

brilliantly staged with a dazzling display of virtuoso showmanship. Chopin's ardent soul, however, is more perfectly expressed in his Ballades, Scherzos, and in some of his Nocturnes, such as that in C-minor, op. 48, no. 1, which is reproduced here (Fig. 103).

Not every listener (nor every player for that matter) may notice that this composition is an example of three-part form. The change from the first section, in C-minor, with its clearly designed melody, to a contrasting middle section in C-major, and with full chords, is easily recognized. Less obvious, however, is the repetition of the first section at the end, because it takes on the form of a variation with the same melody but a completely different accompaniment, the solid and march-like chords of the beginning being replaced by a vibrating background of exciting sonorities. This modification is much more than variety for variety's sake. It has its origin in the middle section where, after the full and sustained chords, an initial stir of excitement is introduced by the quickly reiterated octaves. This agitation quickly gains the upper hand, leading to the thunderous climax at the end of the middle section, and it is from here that it is carried over into the repetition of the first section, as if under the impetus of a tremendous force which cannot suddenly be stopped.

More than any other composer, perhaps with the exception of Bach, Chopin has suffered under the hands of innumerable editors, mostly ambitious virtuosos who, not content with their proper role as concert interpreters, have published their own editions of the works of Chopin. These editions show an appalling lack both of critical judgment and of respect for the composer's intentions. It was not until about ten years ago that the Oxford University Press published an edition of Chopin which, in spite of some serious flaws, ranks high above the others because it presents his works unadulterated by the irresponsible liberties of overbearing virtuosos. It also shows that even the current standard editions, such as those published by Peters or Breitkopf and Härtel, are far from trustworthy. A comparison with the Oxford edition, which, in turn, goes back largely to the French original edition, makes these standard editions appear as the product

103. CHOPIN—*Nocturne*—OP. 48, NO. 1

·245·

of pedantic schoolmasters who were bent on eliminating what appeared to them disorderly irregularities, but what actually are bold and highly interesting peculiarities of Chopin's style. One example may be given here as an illustration. In Chopin's well-known Ballade in A-flat major there is a passage in which a characteristic figure in a slightly syncopated rhythm occurs six times (Fig. 104). The synco-

104.

pated effect is produced by the tying of a note, as in the measures 1, 3, 4, 5, 6, 7 of our example. Actually, only three of these ties are in the original editions, the others being the result of an editorial pedantry. Figure 105 shows the same passage as Chopin wrote it. The artistic superiority of this version is obvious. Compared with its alertness and intensity, the traditional manner of playing sounds insipid. There are numerous passages in many of Chopin's pieces where such ties have been added in the standard editions, resulting in a debilitation of the rhythmic energy and tending to emphasize the perception of Chopin as an effeminate lyricist. Actually, Chopin's musical language is much bolder and much less smoothly conventional than the editions and the majority of the Chopin virtuosos would have us believe.

Brief mention may be made of the important role which Chopin

played in the nineteenth-century development of harmony, a development which led from the prevailingly diatonic harmonies of the classical era to the highly chromatic harmonies of the Romantic. In order to provide a point of departure, a short passage from one of Beethoven's late sonatas, op. 101, may be quoted, a passage which is based upon a chromatic progression of diminished seventh-chords (Fig. 106). While such harmonies strike us as a novelty and exception within the frame of Beethoven's harmonic style, they became the stock-in-trade with the Romantic composers, particularly Chopin and Liszt. A passage from a Chopin Nocturne, op. 32, no. 2, may serve as an illustration (Fig. 107).

Another important trait of Romantic harmony is the frequent use

106.

107.

of rapidly changing harmonies. In classical music the harmony changes relatively slowly, for instance with every measure, or with every half measure, or it may remain unchanged during two measures. The beginning of Beethoven's first piano sonata provides a typical example, showing at the beginning a "harmonic rhythm," as it is called, of two measures, then of one, and finally of half measures (Fig. 108). Beethoven's late works occasionally have passages of an entirely different

108.

harmonic structure: an extremely fast harmonic rhythm, the harmony changing with each of the melody notes. Particularly striking is a passage from his piano sonata "Les Adieux," op. 81a, written in 1811 (Fig. 109) . Harmonic progressions of this type, although exceptional

109.

in Beethoven, are extremely frequent in Chopin. In the passage reproduced here (Fig. 110) , from his Nocturne, op. 62, no. 1, each tone of the melody is accompanied by a new harmony, most of them highly

110.

chromatic. It is interesting to notice that such methods of harmony, familiar and logical as they appear to us, met with violent opposition when they were new. Very likely, Thalberg, one of the conventional drawing-room composers of the early nineteenth century, had such passages in mind when he said: "The worst thing about Chopin is that one does not know at times whether his music is right or wrong." Today it is difficult to understand such criticism, but it is well to remember that criticism in exactly the same words has been leveled against every composer who transgressed the harmonic conventions of his day, against Chopin and Wagner as well as Richard Strauss and Schoenberg.

Felix Mendelssohn (1809–1847) in comparison with Schumann and Chopin, appears as a musical personality of lesser stature. The pleasant ease and sentimentality of his music won him quick fame, and during the second half of the nineteenth century he was by far the most popular of all composers, particularly in England where he became the musical idol of the Victorian era. By reason of this very fact he became suspect to the next generation, and around 1900 he was generally considered and frequently quoted as the typical example of mediocrity. Recently some music writers of high standing have again raised their voices in praise of Mendelssohn, and there can be no doubt that the former depreciation was excessive. One would like to champion his cause, particularly in view of the abuses that have been heaped on him in Hitler-Germany; but in defending him one cannot help feeling like the advocate of a case which, though not without merits, rests on a somewhat weak foundation. Like Mozart, Mendelssohn was a precocious child. In the year 1821, at the age of twelve, he composed five symphonies, nine fugues, two operas, and several other things. Unlike Mozart, however, and somewhat like Schumann, the line of his development took a descending rather than an ascending course or, at best, remained on an even level. Certainly, his most outstanding composition is the overture to Shakespeare's *Midsummer Night's Dream,* written at the age of seventeen. In the field of piano music his fame rests mainly on his Songs Without

Words, forty-eight pieces which he wrote between 1826 and 1845 and which he published in eight books. These are character pieces mostly of the continuous type, that is, without a contrasting middle section. Stylistically they represent a mixture of Romantic and Classical elements—Romantic expression, one might say, cast into the formal language of classicism. Happy though this combination proved with Schubert, it remained somewhat sterile with Mendelssohn, in his Songs Without Words as well as in his symphonies and other works. Those principles of form and design which Haydn, Mozart, Beethoven, and Schubert handled with the superiority of a master, welding them into musical structures of strength, vitality, and flexibility, turned, under the hands of Mendelssohn, into formalistic schemes on which he leaned for support. Nowhere is this more clearly patent than in his melodies which, though pleasing to the untutored ear, are facile and lacking in depth. This fault is aggravated by his musical phraseology which, in many of his compositions, shows a basic design of an obvious and fatal symmetry. His phrases, instead of carrying on the musical thought, simply repeat it under the disguise of changed harmonies. Instead of moving along under their own impulse, they act like a toy balloon that constantly repeats its feeble performance of going up and coming down, although occasionally a wind may carry it a little farther. Almost any of his Songs Without Words serves as an illustration—for instance op. 62, no. 4, shown in Figure 111.

Some English editor of the Victorian era named this piece "Morning Song" and invented similar names for all the others, for instance, "The Evening Star," "The Poet's Harp," or "The Fleecy Cloud." May Mendelssohn's magnanimous and kindly soul forgive him for this well-meant but ill-considered service by which he put the works of an important composer in the same class with the "Prayer of a Virgin" or the "Joyous Sleighride." Mendelssohn *is* an important composer in spite of his faults and weaknesses; he is not a star of the first order, but at least he has one virtue which is rather rare among the companions of his rank, the virtue of modesty, the virtue of not simulating a greatness which is not his. Indeed, a piece such as the one I

111. MENDELSSOHN—*Song Without Words*—OP. 62, NO. 4

just cited possesses a certain charm of unpretentiousness which, one may feel, outweighs its flaws. Nevertheless, it seems to me that the discussion of any work of art should always proceed from the highest level, that is, from the assumption that it is meant to be a work of the highest rank. I wonder whether we should accept the view, rather widespread among writers and critics, that there are different standards of artistic judgment, one for Beethoven and his kind, another for Mendelssohn, and yet another for Smith and Jones. Music is not a shop where one customer may buy the first quality of wool for the highest price, while another may make just as good a buy in second-grade wool at a lower price.

Although flaws of the type described above are sufficiently frequent in Mendelssohn to be considered a basic trait of his style, there are a number of his compositions in which he rises to greater heights of artistic significance. This is the case with three pieces in particular, among the Songs Without Words, where the inspiration came from outside, from the songs of the Venetian gondoliers. The last of these three pieces, "Venetian Boatsong," op. 62, no. 5, is given here (Fig. 112) in order to show what Mendelssohn could achieve when he was able to free himself from his own conventions.

We finally turn to a brief consideration of the last member of the group of early Romanticists, the Hungarian-born Franz Liszt (1811–1886). Actually, it is not quite correct to call him an "early" Romanticist, since his long span of life, extending thirty years beyond that of Schumann, Chopin, and Mendelssohn, gives him a place among the "middle" as well as among the "early" Romanticists, side by side with Brahms, Tchaikovsky, and others.

Liszt, as a composer, is one of the most controversial figures of nineteenth-century music. Condemned by many as a mere charlatan, he has been praised by others as a great genius. In a way he is both. His works are just as full of inspired and fascinating ideas as they are of cheap and superficial tinsel. Many of his pieces begin like a revelation and end like a circus show. At any rate, he is not given full justice if he is judged only by his most spectacular pieces, such as the Hungarian

Rhapsodies or the Transcendental Etudes. He is at his best in his more lyrical compositions, for example, some of the Sonetti di Petrarca, and particularly some of his latest works which are almost completely unknown, for instance, his "Second Elegy," written in 1878 (Fig. 113).

113. LISZT—*Second Elegy*

sempre appassionato ed un poco accel.

Although the musical quality of Liszt's piano compositions is open to debate, there is no question about the central position they hold in the development of modern pianism. A most interesting illustration of what Liszt contributed in this field is provided by a little-known collection of pieces which he published in 1826 under the title of *Etudes en forme de douze exercises*. In glancing through this slender volume one is surprised by the appearance of its contents, which look like Czerny or Cramer rather than Liszt. Even more surprising, however, is the discovery that these harmless looking and harmless sounding pieces are the forerunners of those twelve etudes which he published thirty years later, in 1852, under the eminently justified title *Etudes d'execution transcendentale*—Etudes of Transcendent Execution—compositions which indeed transcend in technical difficulty anything written before or after. Actually, these etudes are not a second, but a third version, since the same pieces had appeared in 1837, under title of *Grandes études*. Reproduced here are three versions for the beginning of one of these etudes, the one which in the final edition is inscribed "Mazeppa," in memory of that famous seventeenth-century Cossack hetman (Fig. 114).

In 1853, three years before his death, Robert Schumann, in his last article, introduced to the musical world a new composer, then twenty years of age, greeting him with the words: "We bid him welcome as a forceful fighter." This young composer was Johannes Brahms (1833–1897), and among the compositions which caused this prophetic remark was his opus 1, a piano sonata in C-major (Fig. 115). This sonata shows a fiery enthusiasm, a bold daring, which immediately recall Beethoven, and we may well understand that, at the time when the blue flower of Romanticism was already wilting away, this composition was greeted as the herald of a new era of vigorous life.

Strangely enough, the youthful exuberance of Brahms's opus 1 subsided rather quickly, giving way to an introspective lyricism, to a meditative, and even hesitating, pensiveness which led in a somewhat different direction. Two more piano sonatas of a highly dramatic character, op. 2 and op. 5, were written in the same year as the first,

and the truly magnificent Piano Concerto in D-minor followed in the next year, but thereafter he veered more and more toward a style in which the dynamic and dramatic elements, though by no means lacking, appear as the result of deliberate efforts rather than of immediate impulses. His late works for the pianoforte, ranging from op. 71 to op. 119, and written between 1871 and 1892, are all Romantic character pieces in that typically Brahmsian idiom of somber hues

115. BRAHMS—*Sonata*—OP. 1

and subdued emotions, of fading light and half-weary resignation.

A music critic once said of Brahms that he wrote one-thousand-and-one lullabies, a witticism which contains a good deal of truth. Any number of themes and melodies in his compositions show a typical design of zigzag contours, moving gently back and forth and deliberately avoiding direction. The main theme of his Fourth Symphony is a significant example (Fig. 116).

116.

Another characteristic trait of Brahms's musical style is his penchant for parallel sixths and thirds which are used as a sort of sonorous ground-color for many melodies, a technique which, in a way, might be considered as the forerunner of Debussy's parallel harmonies. The Intermezzo, op. 116, no. 4 (Fig. 117), shows both these features, the lullaby character in the first theme, the parallel sixths and thirds in the second.

1900 – IMPRESSIONISM AND NEW MUSIC – 1940

THE SUBJECT OF THIS CHAPTER, the last of our series, is the piano-forte music of the twentieth century. While this is, in a way, the most interesting topic of our study, it is also by far the most difficult. Aside from the fact that in any field and at any time the study of the present offers problems essentially different from and more intricate than those involved in the investigation of the past, the particular matter in hand is a phenomenon of such complexity as is not found in any other period of music history. The mere number of composers who have taken an active part in the development of twentieth-century music far exceeds that in any period of comparable length. It seems as though, around 1900, the social structure of music had undergone a radical change, leading from an oligarchic to a democratic organization, from the rule of a few to the participation of the broad masses. Naturally, this picture as we see it today is not wholly objective in the historical sense. Very likely, future history will eliminate from the scene a great number of men who appear to us as players of important roles, much in the same way as it eliminated from the period of Beethoven such names as Wölfl, Hüttenbrenner, and Ries.

To the complexity caused by the sheer multitude of names is added that resulting from the diversity and incongruity of activities represented. In this respect the music of the twentieth century presents a picture the like of which is not encountered elsewhere. The decade from 1910 to 1920 in particular is characterized by a confusing variety of efforts and tendencies. Last but not least, the complete novelty of the various methods and styles, as well as their technical intricacy, greatly adds to the difficulty involved in a study and presentation of present-day music.

Fortunately, the multiformity of the phenomenon is one of appearance rather than of basic trends. Varied and conflicting though the efforts of present-day composers appear to the baffled listener, they are just so many different phases of one fundamental reaction which can be summed up in the word "anti-romanticism."

By virtue of its origin as well as of its main line of growth, the Romantic movement in music was always considered, and justly so, an essentially German movement, notwithstanding the coöperation it received from a few non-German composers, like Chopin, Liszt, and Tchaikovsky. But the very prominence of the German element, a prominence which, to be sure, started long before Romanticism with Bach, Haydn, Mozart, and Beethoven, was bound to lead, sooner or later, to a reaction. The first embodiment of the rising revolt against German supremacy in music was the movement known as nationalism, a movement which emphasized the resources of national folklore, folk melody, and folk dance as a factor of musical inspiration and which for the first time brought nations such as Norway, Spain, Bohemia, and so on into the center of musical life. This is not the place to evaluate this movement which, on the whole, found a more convincing expression in operas and symphonic poems than in compositions for the pianoforte. Of greater interest to us is the attack against German Romanticism which was launched, shortly before 1900, in France by Claude Debussy (1862–1918) and which led to the establishment of a new musical style known as Impressionism. Like musical nationalism, the Impressionist movement was rooted in antagonism, but, in contrast to the champions of nationalism, Debussy showed enough ingenuity to combat the Germans by purely musical weapons, by methods which, though very "French" in character, are free from nationalistic motives or ramifications. Debussy instinctively disliked the dramatic dynamism of Beethoven, the erotic ecstasy of the Wagnerian operas, and the exuberant emotionalism of the Romanticists in general. The novel technique of the French Impressionistic painters, such as Monet, Manet, and Renoir, as well as the refined poetry of Verlaine, Baudelaire, and Mallarme suggested to him a new type of music, a music which seems to hint rather than to state; in which a succession of colors take the place of dynamic development, and atmospheric sensations supersede heroic pathos; a music which is as vague and intangible as the changing lights of the day, as the subtle noises of the wind and the rain.

Debussy not only conceived the idea of a new kind of music, but also established the technical basis necessary to put this idea into reality. Completely abandoning the traditional forms of the symphony and sonata, he adopted the short program piece as his favored vehicle of expression, or, rather, of impression. Indeed, while to the Romantic mind music was the expression of the inner self, Debussy conceived of it as a supersensitive mirror reflecting the impressions received from the outer world, an outer world, to be sure, not of hard facts and stark realities, but of subtle shades and vague contours. His antithetic attitude towards musical Romanticism also appears in a number of novel devices of composition which are in direct opposition to the established principles of nineteenth-century harmony and melody. Two of these devices may be mentioned here: parallel chords and the whole-tone scale.

Parallel chords (Fig. 118) means the successive sounding of a fixed chordal combination, consonant or dissonant, on various degrees of the

118.

scale; a procedure which obviously results in a parallel movement for all the constituent tones of the chord. In classical harmony this method is admissible only for chords which involve no other intervals than thirds and sixths, for instance the sixth chord, 1–3–6 (a), which was used in the fauxbourdon of the fifteenth century, and the third or sixth with doubled octave, 1–3–8 or 1–6–8, which Brahms was so fond of (b, c). It is, however, strictly forbidden for triads (d), seventh chords (e), and so forth, because of the parallel fifths which would result in these cases. In deliberate violation of these principles, Debussy made ample use of parallelism for triads and seventh chords, as well as for any dissonant combination, involving seconds, fourths, and so on. Figure 119 shows a few typical examples of Debussy's parallel harmony.

119.

This harmonic idiom is in opposition to traditional harmony not only because it violates the rule against parallel fifths or because it introduces unresolved dissonances, but even more so because it rejects that fundamental principle of traditional harmony which may be termed its functional character. In an example like that shown in Figure 120, each chord is clearly felt to have individual significance

120.

as well as its proper position within a well-defined entity. These properties are entirely lost in a parallel-chord formation in which the chords, being all essentially alike, lose their individual character and assume the role of a purely sonorous phenomenon.

Another characteristic trait of Debussy's style is the rather frequent use of the whole-tone scale (Fig. 121), that is, a scale consisting of six

121.

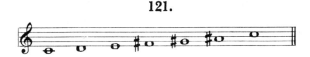

whole tones, while the traditional scale consists of seven tones, five whole tones and two semi-tones. The whole-tone scale lacks three of the most fundamental intervals of traditional music: the perfect fifth (c–g), the perfect fourth (c–f), and the semitone leading up to the octave b–c'). Moreover, owing to the equality of all its steps it lacks that attribute of localization and centralization which in the traditional scales is indicated by the terms "tonic," "dominant," "subdominant," and so forth. It is interesting to notice that parallel chords and the whole-tone scale, although of an entirely different nature, bear a certain fundamental relationship to each other. Both idioms signify the characteristic trend of Impressionism to eliminate functional differentiations, to replace vitality of texture by variety of color, and dynamic forces by sonorous plains.

The beginning of Debussy's "Sarabande," composed about 1900, is reproduced here (Fig. 122) * as an example of his earlier style.

While in his earlier compositions for the pianoforte Debussy tends towards massive and occasionally somewhat ostentatious sonorities, he preferred, in his later works, paler colors and a "silk-brush" technique resulting in what has been termed "tonal envelopes" or "sound-wraiths." A good example is a composition written in 1907 and entitled, with his typical flair for refinement and sophistication, "Et la

---

* Permission granted by Durand Cie., Paris, France, and Elkan-Vogel Co., Inc., Philadelphia, Pa. Copyright Owners.

122. DEBUSSY—*Sarabande*

lune descend sur le temple qui fut"—And the moon descends on the temple that was— (Fig. 123) .*

*Permission granted by Durand Cie., Paris, France, and Elkan-Vogel Co., Inc., Philadelphia, Pa., Copyright Owners.

123. DEBUSSY—*Et la lune descend sur le temple qui fut*

Impressionism, in spite of the sensation it created, after a relatively short time began to lose much of its original fascination. Its intrinsic vagueness and over-refinement were not conducive to vigorous development. It is a somewhat tragic truth that Debussy's work stands before the eye of the present-day viewer not as what he intended, the negation of Romanticism, but as a part thereof, in fact, its very acme and conclusion. His fundamental point of view, however, was shared by other composers who were equally convinced that the potentialities of the Romantic approach had been exploited to the very limit, technically as well as aesthetically, and that new solutions had to be found, solutions, however, of a more decisive and radical nature than his. Such solutions were indeed found by men like Schoenberg, Bartok, Stravinsky, and Hindemith, and the novelty and radicalism of their efforts are properly indicated by the term "New Music" which has gradually come into acceptance as a designation for the progressive tendencies in the music of the early twentieth century. This term has a more limited and, therefore, more accurate meaning than "Modern Music" or "Contemporary Music" insofar as it excludes composers like Sibelius or Richard Strauss, who continued more or less along the traditional lines of the late nineteenth century, expounding the ideas and technical resources of Romanticism, Impressionism, nationalism, and so on. It may be noticed that the term New Music also has an interesting historical significance, as it recalls similar names which were used in earlier periods for movements of a somewhat similar character: *Ars nova* (New art) and *Nuove musiche* (New music). Particularly interesting is the fact that these movements occurred at intervals of exactly three hundred years, the *Ars nova* around 1300, the *Nuove musiche* around 1600, and the New Music around 1900. Whether one accepts these dates as a mere coincidence, or interprets them as the expression of an innate law of musical evolution, they are useful as landmarks, and they also remind us that an occasional break in tradition is no more less natural to historical development than is continuity and steady growth.

In order to understand the break of tradition which occurred around 1900 it must be realized that Romanticism meant to its opponents two things, one of an ideological, the other of a technical, character. The former of these two aspects is nineteenth-century subjectivism, the latter, nineteenth-century harmony. This distinction is reflected in the activity of the anti-romanticists, some of whom strove mainly for ideological renovation, while others worked towards the establishment of novel technical means.

As far as the opposition against subjectivism and exuberant emotionalism is concerned, the initiative was taken primarily by the French Erik Satie (1866–1925) and the Italo-German Ferruccio Busoni (1866–1924). As early as 1890 Satie wrote pieces which held up to ridicule the exhibitionism and ostentatiousness of the late Romanticism and the *fin-de-siècle* refinement of Impressionism; these works, though artistically insignificant and trifling, clearly show the new tendency to revolt. His novel methods are startling rather than convincing: he omits bar-lines; he makes sophisticated use of a simple C-major instead of the piled-up chromaticism of Richard Strauss and Debussy; he coins absurd titles such as "Pièces en forme de poire" (Pieces in the Shape of a Pear), "Embryons dessêchés" (Desiccated Embryos), or "Véritables préludes flasques pour un chien" (Veritable Flaccid Preludes for a Dog); and he replaces the traditional expression marks by plainly satiric directions such as *Comme un rossignol qui a mal de dent* (Like a nightingale with a toothache). These methods are significant, not as such, but as indications of a mentality which was bent on shocking the bourgeois, including the bourgeois musician. Busoni's opposition to Romanticism was of a quite different and much more serious nature; it was determined by his "German" congeniality to Bach and Mozart, and by his "Italian" penchant for the eighteenth-century comedy with its dry and unsentimental buffoonery. These tendencies make him the father of the most important current of New Music: neo-classicism, which we shall consider later in more detail.

Prominent among the men who finally broke the fetters of nineteenth-century harmony were the Russian Alexander Scriabin (1872–

1915) and the Austrian Arnold Schoenberg (b. 1874). Scriabin, although spiritually a highly Romantic individualist and mystic, worked untiringly toward novel principles of harmony. Around 1910 he arrived at a harmonic system based, not on consecutive thirds which form the basis of all triads and therefore of traditional harmony, but on consecutive fourths. Entire compositions of his are derived from chords such as those shown in Figure 124.

124.

Scriabin wrote a great number of compositions for the pianoforte, and it is very interesting to compare one of his earlier pieces, called "Album Leaf," op. 45, no. 1 (Fig. 125), written in 1903, with one of his latest, a "Prélude," op. 74 (Fig. 126), written in 1914. There is little room for doubt as to which of these compositions is more interesting historically, and, at the same time, more significant artistically. The first is one of those dime-a-dozen pieces in which worn-out clichés of chromatic harmony and cheaply sentimental melody are once more pressed to the last drop in an attempt to bring about some semblance of originality and novelty. The second is an extremely bold attempt to work with new tools, and, at the same time, a typical example of Scriabin's efforts to put into musical reality that mystic ecstasy which took complete possession of his mind in the later years of his life.

Novel and radical though the musical style of Scriabin's prelude appears to the listener of today, thirty years after it was written, it was not radical enough to constitute that complete break with tradition which the musical pioneers of the early twentieth century deemed necessary. It is generally conceded that this break occurred with the publication, in 1909, of Arnold Schoenberg's *Drei Klavierstücke* (Three Pieces for the Pianoforte), op. 11. From the harmonic point of view the difference between these pieces and those by Scriabin is that Scriabin's, although they employ striking dissonances and completely discard the triadic basis of harmony, nevertheless retain tonality, that fundamental principle of all music written before our time.

125. SCRIABIN—*Album Leaf*

This tonality is not, of course, in the traditional sense of major and minor tonality composed of triads, seventh chords, and their numerous derivatives, but in the most general connotation of the term as,

126. SCRIABIN—*Prélude*

to quote the definition given by Vincent d'Indy, "the ensemble of musical phenomena which can be appreciated by direct comparison with a constant element—the tonic." The existence of a tonic or, as one may call it, tonal center, is clearly noticeable in Scriabin's prelude which has the tone f-sharp as its tonal center, although its harmonic style is essentially different from that of a composition in F-sharp major or minor. Schoenberg, in his opus 11 and even more so in his *Sechs kleine Klavierstücke* (Six Little Piano Pieces) , op. 16, cast away the last vestiges of tonality, thus establishing a new harmonic—or, rather, unharmonic—style: atonality.

The principle of atonality is the use of the twelve tones of the chromatic scale as elements having equal rights, that is, without making any of them the center of reference. Taking this definition as a point of departure, the question arises as to the very existence of atonal music; in fact, it has been repeatedly maintained that atonal music is contradictory in itself, in other words, that music, consisting of tones, necessarily must show relationships between these tones, relationships by which one tone assumes, at least for the moment, the position of a central tone. Such an argument is, however, too mathematically correct to be artistically true. Tonal relationships, in the musical sense, are not a matter of demonstrable facts, but a matter of intentions on the part of the composer. While it is impossible to avoid all tonal relationships in writing music, it is entirely possible to write music with a complete disregard of tonal relationships, and this is exactly what Schoenberg did. The result of this most radical step is as startling and shocking today as it was thirty-five years ago, as the reproduced example, No. V of the *Sechs kleine Klavierstücke* (Fig. 127) ,* will readily show.

As has previously been pointed out, the novelty of these pieces lies in their technical aspect rather than in their aesthetic or ideological quality. Considered from this last point of view, they show a subjectivism and emotionalism reminiscent of that of the Romantic compos-

* By permission of Arnold Schoenberg and Associated Music Publishers, Inc., New York, N. Y. Copyright Owners.

127. SCHOENBERG—*Sechs kleine Klavierstücke, V*

ers, although differing from this somewhat in the same way as psycho-analysis differs from psychology. Nevertheless, to emphasize this aspect by calling Schoenberg a Romantic composer—as is frequently done —is misleading, all the more since his later development has led him far from Romanticism toward a highly intellectual constructivism. Realizing that the postulate of atonality was hardly more than a negation, he began to search for constructive principles of organization to be used in the place of the conventional principles of triadic harmony. The result of this search was his so-called twelve-tone technique, which he employed for the first time in his Serenade, op. 24, of 1923, and in his Piano Suite, op. 25, of 1924.

The basic principle of this rather involved technique is the use of a tone-row, that is, an arbitrary arrangement of the twelve chromatic tones, for instance that shown in Figure 128; these tones serve as the

128.

exclusive thematic substance for the entire composition. This means that the composition consists structurally of nothing but restatements of the tone-row, either in its original form or in one of the various modifications which can be obtained by means of inversion, retrograde motion, and transposition, the total number of these modifications being forty-eight. In the subsequent example the original tone-row is designated by the letter T, while Tr indicates its retrograde form (that is, read backwards), Ti its inverted form (that is, turned upside down), and Tri the inversion of the retrograde form (Fig. 129). Since each of these four forms can be transposed to any of the twelve keys, there result forty-eight modifications of the original tone-row.

Naturally, each of these tone-rows, although fixed as to the arrangement of its constituent tones, leads to an unlimited number of musical formations through two additional elements of variety—rhythm and

129.

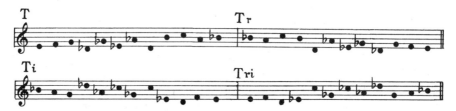

chordal grouping. This may be illustrated by the Trio from Schoenberg's Suite, op. 25 (Fig. 130) ,* which is based on the tone-row given above.

In the first two systems the tone-row appears three times as a purely melodic formation, as indicated by the letters T and Ti. In the third system a more complex method is used, the details of which will appear from the figures 1 to 12 given with the various notes. It may be noticed that in the two last statements, on system four, the position of the tones 7 and 8 is reversed.[37]

One cannot help being impressed by the radical novelty of Schoenberg's ideas, and the boldness and inexorability with which he pursues these ideas to an uncompromising solution. But it is not easy, even with the best of intentions, to accept this solution as an artistic reality. The fact that Schoenberg's compositions are dissonant, much more so indeed than those of any other composer, is irrelevant in this connection, as there is no reason why great music may not be written in a dissonant idiom as well as in a consonant or semi-consonant style. A more serious objection is presented by the fact that his compositions are deliberately constructed, constructed to such an extent that a sixteenth-century ricercare appears by comparison a free flight of fancy. Indeed it is doubtful whether the rigidity of the twelve-tone technique leaves enough room or provides a sufficiently strong stimulus for artistic imagination. It should be noticed, however, that more recently Schoenberg and one of his followers, Ernst Křenek, have treated the principles of twelve-tone technique with considerably

* By permission of Arnold Schoenberg and Associated Music Publishers, Inc., New York, N. Y. Copyright Owners.

130. SCHOENBERG—*Trio from Suite*—OP. 25

greater freedom. At any rate, Schoenberg's music and his piano style in particular should not be judged on the basis of his piano compositions alone. The piano parts of his *Pierrot Lunaire,* of the suite for three clarinets, three strings, and piano, and of the concerto for piano and orchestra should be studied in order to obtain a complete picture of his contributions in the field of present-day piano music.

At about the same time as Schoenberg made his first ventures in atonality, another potent factor appeared on the musical scene—rhythm. Rhythm not in the conventional sense as the accessory scheme of note values and accents as which, of course, it is present in music of all times, but as a primary and generating element of musical life. While in European music rhythm had always been relegated to the role of a servant, a different situation exists in the music of the primitive races; the African Negroes, in particular, have preserved to the present day that aboriginal state of affairs, antedating the invention of melody instruments, in which drums are the only means of producing sounds. As in the early years of the twentieth century French painters became fascinated by the symbolic ugliness of aboriginal Negro art, so musicians began to listen to the weird sounds of the Dark Continent. Probably the earliest example of this influence in piano literature is a composition of the Hungarian composer Béla Bartók (1881–1945), called "Allegro Barbaro" (1910), written in a truly barbaric style. Figure 131 * shows the beginning of this exciting composition.

This new percussive style evoked enthusiastic response in many quarters of the musical world where it was considered as a more positive and constructive contribution than Schoenberg's atonality. The very spirit of decadence which pervaded European culture in the years before World War I provided a favorable atmosphere for what one may call a twentieth-century *retour à la nature.* The French essayist Jean Cocteau, looking back at the Impressionism of Debussy and Ravel, aptly summed up the new situation in the famous words: "After the music with the silk brush, the music with the axe." From

* By permission of the copyright owners, Hawkes & Son (London) Ltd. Copyright 1918. Renewed 1945.

131. BARTÓK—*Allegro Barbaro*

the music inspired by the drums of the African jungle it was only a small step to the music of the modern machines, and in 1912 the Futurist writer Francesco Pratello somewhat boastfully described the music of the future in the following words: "To express the musical soul of the masses, of the great industrial ship-yards, of the railways, steamboats, battleships, automobiles and aeroplanes; to add to the great central idea of the musical poem the province of the machine, and the victorious empire of electricity." Composers like Arthur Honegger (b. 1892), Darius Milhaud (b. 1892), and Francis Poulenc (b. 1899) have translated into musical language the relentless mechanistic motion of the modern machines.

After World War I the music of rhythm received a fresh impetus through the importation into Europe of American jazz. In 1917 and 1918 American jazz bands were heard for the first time in Paris and created a sensation not only among dance enthusiasts, but also among the progressive-minded composers who eagerly seized upon the possibilities offered by the exciting rhythms and bold syncopations of ragtime, the foxtrot, shimmy, and so on. From 1918 to 1930 a great number of pieces were written which show the rhythmic style of jazz dances cleverly combined with the strongly dissonant style which at that time had already been accepted as a basic idiom, and which, debatable though some of its merits may be, possesses undeniable advantages if music of a strongly percussive character is desired. One only has to play the chords shown in Figure 132 under (a) and (b) in order to make this unpleasant fact clear.

132.

An interesting reflection of the jazz period in art music is a suite by Paul Hindemith (b. 1895) entitled *1922,* and consisting of five movements which are a vivid memorial of those days when the whole of Europe, whether victorious or defeated, was in a state of mental turbulence and desperation which threw the doors open to jazz and expressionism as well as to communism and theosophy. The last of the movements in Hindemith's suite, called "Ragtime," is accompanied by a "Direction for Use" which sets forth the intentions of the composer as follows: "Forget what you have learned in your piano lesson. Don't trouble whether to play D-sharp with the fourth or the sixth finger. Play this piece recklessly, but always rigidly in rhythm like a machine. Consider the piano as a sort of percussion instrument and act accordingly." More readily attractive is the fourth movement of this suite, called "Boston," [38] a strange mixture of subdued eroticism and ecstatic pathos. Even more impressive is the dream vision of the "Nachtstück," one of the numerous pieces by Hindemith in which use is made of the ostinato technique.[39]

Yet another characteristic trait in the spotted picture of the music of this period is the tendency toward derision and satire. Not so long ago there was a time when writers of philosophical dissertations were able to "prove" that music had the distinction of affording no place for satire and caricature. Whether we like it or not, the past thirty years have brought forth abundant evidence to the contrary. The subtly ironic nature of Erik Satie's compositions has been pointed out previously. More clearly satirical are pieces in which the disharmonic idiom of twentieth-century music is used as a means of deliberate distortion. More than any other subject, the dances of the Victorian era, the wáltz and the polka, have become the target of mockery, as for instance in the waltz (Fig. 133) * from Igor Stravinsky's *Histoire du soldat,* a ballet written in 1918.

Satire, jazz, machine music, barbarism, atonality—these are some of the motley ingredients out of which the picture of the post-Impressionistic period is formed, a period as unruly and anarchic as there ever was in music history. There was bound to come a time when revolution for its own sake was to give way to forces of a more constructive and positive nature, when the purely antithetical tendencies were to be replaced by efforts leading to a new synthesis. This change took place around 1920 when, after so many futile experiments and contradictory solutions, a new name appeared on the scene: Bach. This was the magic word which proved strong enough to dispel the destructive

* Permission granted by J. & W. Chester Ltd., 11, Great Marlborough Street, London, W. 1, Copyright Owners.

133. STRAVINSKY—*Valse*

instincts, to make an end to short-lived sensations, and to unite practically all the prominent composers in a new spirit of seriousness and constructive coöperation. Around or after 1920 they all entered what is usually termed their third period, that is to say, the "neo-classical" period after the "impressionistic" and the "anarchic." From the point of view of progress and evolution it might seem regrettable that, after all the radicalism of the previous years, music had to turn back to "history" in order to proceed to a new future. Yet, evolution or progress, whatever we call it, does not always proceed in a straight line, certainly not in the arts. A situation somewhat similar to that of the present day existed in music three hundred years ago, when the radicalism of monody, as represented in the early operas by Caccini, Peri, and Monteverdi, was tempered by the reintegration of elements of the contrapuntal Renaissance music, a perfect example of Hegelian synthesis after the thesis and the antithesis. The music of the twentieth century shows essentially the same evolutionary structure, but with a noteworthy difference, insofar as here the synthesis was achieved by reverting to a period much earlier than that which had served as the point of departure. In fact, throughout the development of New Music, Romanticism and all it stands for remained taboo, and only in some works of a very recent date can a somewhat more tolerant attitude in this matter be observed.

The return to Bach, which is the characteristic earmark of neo-classicism, led to the revival of early forms such as the suite, the toccata, the passacaglia, the ricercare, the invention, the concerto grosso, and the basso ostinato. It led to a new style of detachment and objectivity, often deliberately dry and unexpressive. Above all, it led to an emphasis on contrapuntal texture, in contrast to the harmonic structure of Romantic music and the prevailingly rhythmic and percussive structure of the intermediate period. Naturally, modern counterpoint sounds quite different from that of Bach. Bach's counterpoint, as well as that of Palestrina and all the other early masters, is consonant counterpoint, which means that the voice parts, although individually designed, nevertheless conform with the principles of consonance and harmony. Modern counterpoint is a dissonant type in which the harmonic requirement is no longer recognized. The short tune which has been used in one of the previous chapters (p. 175) to demonstrate the difference between harmonic and contrapuntal style may also be used to illustrate the difference between the old and the new type of counterpoint (Fig. 134). In order to change our example

134.

of consonant counterpoint (a) into one of dissonant or, as it is sometimes called, "reckless" counterpoint, we only have to play the lower part one step higher, as under (b). Yet another possibility, no less reckless and shocking, is to transpose the lower part a second upward, into the key of D-major, as under (c).

These examples of modern counterpoint illustrate two important methods of composition frequently encountered in the works of contemporary composers, and known as pandiatonicism and bitonality. The term pandiatonicism is composed of the Greek word *pan* (all, everything), and diatonic, the traditional term for music which is non-chromatic, that is to say, which uses only the tones of the C-major scale, or any other major or minor scale. It indicates what one may call an "anything-goes" attitude towards the C-major scale; the principle of atonality is applied to the seven white keys instead of, as with Schoenberg, to the twelve chromatic keys. This analogy, however, holds good only from the methodical point of view. Historically, pandiatonicism is neither a modification nor a continuation of atonality, but a reaction against the chromaticism of the preceding decades, whether atonal, as in the case of Schoenberg, or tonal, as in the case of Debussy. In fact, a page from, for example, Stravinsky's *Serenade*, written in 1925, with its appearance of an innocent C-major offers a most striking contrast to the piling up of sharps and flats in a page from Debussy or Schoenberg. It is, however, far from sounding as harmless as it looks. In the following passages from Stravinsky's *Sérénade en La* (first movement, "Hymne") we find an example of a pandiatonic F-major (a) and one involving modulation (b) from A-major to C-major (Fig. 135).*

135.

The pandiatonic style is even more fully realized in one of Stravinsky's most recent compositions, a sonata for two pianos (1945). Its second movement is a theme with variations, and variation 4 (Fig. 136),† is a characteristic example of present-day D-major.

Other composers, particularly of the modern French school, have

* By permission of Edition Russe de Musique and the Galaxy Music Corporation, New York, N. Y. Copyright Owners.
† By permission of Associated Music Publishers, Inc., and Chappell & Co. Inc., New York, N. Y. Copyright Owners.

136. STRAVINSKY—*Sonata for Two Pianos, Variation 4*

VARIATION 4
conclusion

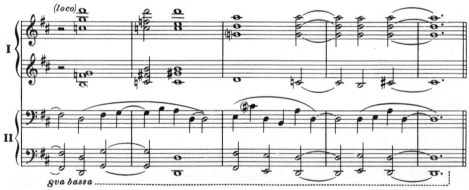

used the pandiatonic idiom in a more pleasant and obliging manner. Francis Poulenc, for instance, has written a considerable number of pieces which sound like a modernized, and somewhat trivialized, Mozart or Schubert. The beginning of the first number of a collection called *Mouvements perpétuels* is reproduced here (Fig. 137).*

Bitonality is, as the name implies, the simultaneous use of two different tonalities or keys, for instance, C-major in the right hand

* By permission of J. & W. Chester Ltd., 11, Great Marlborough Street, London, W. 1. Copyright Owners.

137. POULENC—*Mouvements perpétuels*

against D-major in the left hand. Among the earliest examples of this technique are passages in Stravinsky's *Petrouchka* (1911) in which the right hand uses the white keys of C-major, the left hand the black keys of F-sharp major, a combination which is known as the "Petrouchka

138.

chord" (Fig. 138). This "black-and-white" technique offers, of course, unlimited possibilities for musical jokes, for instance that shown in Figure 139.

139.

The neo-classical school has found an outstanding representative in Paul Hindemith. The period of negation, irony, and dance madness affected him no less deeply than other composers, but he emerged from it with an astounding resilience and vitality. Shortly after 1922 he found his personal interpretation of neo-classicism, and ever since he has pursued his path with a directness and consistency which offer a striking contrast to the rather unpredictable career of Stravinsky. In fact, his working in an established style has earned him the reproach of lack of originality and inventiveness, all the more since he has repeatedly declared himself in accord with that current school of thought which favors a craftsman-like attitude towards the business of composition. It may be well to remember, however, that similar traits are found in the work of Bach and of the early composers in general, and that not until the nineteenth century did originality and sudden inspiration begin to be thought of as necessary implements of the creative artist.

Hindemith's musical temperament is far removed from trickery and sophistication, and his every work of the past twenty years bears the imprint of a natural vitality which expresses itself equally well in dynamic vigor and in lyrical tenderness. Particularly significant is his activity in the field of the sonata, a form which was almost ostentatiously neglected by the other composers of the New Music movement. His three pianoforte sonatas, written in 1936, are among the few really important examples written after Schubert, and certainly are among the most outstanding contributions to the literature of the instrument which have been made during the past fifty years. One may feel that here, at last, we have arrived at that synthesis of progressive and traditional elements on which a new and lasting future of music may be built. Reproduced here (Fig. 140) * is the first movement of the first of Hindemith's three sonatas.[40]

Today more than ever during its evolution music stands at the crossroads. The turmoil which accompanied the most recent phase of this evolution has not yet subsided, and nobody can as yet foretell in what direction the path of the future will lead. It may well lead to a new period of great art, or it may lead to deterioration and stagnation. The responsibility for this decision rests with the composers of our day—but not exclusively so. It also rests, and to a great extent, with the public. Is the public prepared to give full support to those who are striving seriously for a great new future of music, or is it rather inclined to lend a willing ear to the charlatans and providers of cheap entertainment who are so plentiful in our midst? One cannot help having some doubt in this matter, and I may be permitted to say that my personal feeling of doubt and apprehension has been par-

* Permission granted by Associated Music Publishers, Inc., New York, N. Y. Copyright Owners.

ticularly aroused by the phenomenal success of a recent composition, originally written for a film. I would gladly grant its excellence within this province which naturally caters to popular success, but instead of finding its well-deserved place of honor on top of the inevitable pile of song-hits, it has in innumerable homes and minds found its way into the company of Tchaikovsky and Debussy, not to say of Bach and Beethoven. How it has been possible for this suavely conventional and cheaply entertaining after-dinner music to deceive, not only the millions of people to whom music is always an after-dinner affair, but also thousands of musical amateurs of taste and cultural standing, is an enigma which we certainly shall not bother to solve. At any rate, it is a most alarming token of a trend which, if encouraged and strengthened, may well lead to a complete destruction of music as an art. Let us all hope that such apprehension is unfounded. Let us all work together so that this country may emerge as a world center, not only of economic and political power, of scientific research and technical progress, but also of the humanities and the arts, and that music may find her proper place among them.

NOTES

HDM stands for the *Harvard Dictionary of Music,* edited by Willi Apel (Cambridge: Harvard University Press, 1944).

1. The titles of these books are, respectively: *Quatorze gaillardes, neuf pavanes* (Attaingnant, 1530) ; *Intabulatura nova di varie sorte de balli* (1551) ; Francesco Bendusi, *Opera nova de balli* (1553).

2. Vita S. Swithuni; see Francis Diederich Wackerbarth, *Music and the Anglo-Saxons* (London: W. Pickering, 1837), pp. 12–15.

3. The so-called Squarcialupi Codex, Florence, Bibl. Laur., *Pal.* 87.

4. In America, the pioneer of this movement is G. Donald Harrison of the Aeolian-Skinner Company, Boston; Harrison built the Baroque organ which is in the Germanic Museum of Harvard University, and on which radio performances are given every Sunday.

5. See the article on "Echiquier" in *HDM.* For additional information on the history of various keyboard instruments, see Curt Sachs, *The History of Musical Instruments* (New York: W. W. Norton & Company, 1940).

6. Sebastian Virdung, *Musica getutscht* (Music in the German Language) published in Basle in 1511. A modern edition of this work was published by Breitkopf and Härtel in 1882.

7. This refers to Johann Christian Bach (1735–1782), Johann Sebastian Bach's youngest son, also known as the "London" or "Milanese" Bach (see p. 191).

8. Brit. Mus., *Add. 28550.*

9. Reproduced, by kind permission of the publishers, from Willi Apel, *Musik aus früher Zeit* (Mainz and Leipzig: B. Schott's Söhne [1934]). This book is a collection of compositions illustrating the development of keyboard music during the Middle Ages and the Renaissance period. The Figures 11, 17, 19, 37, 39, and 41 are from the same collection.

10. Examples illustrating the development of early vocal music are found in Arnold Schering, *Geschichte der Musik in Beispielen* (Leipzig: Breitkopf and Härtel, 1931), and in A. T. Davison and Willi Apel,

Historical Anthology of Music (Cambridge: Harvard University Press, 1946).

11. Free rhythm prevails in the upper parts of the two-voice compositions (*organa dupla*) of the school of St. Martial, *c.* 1150. Shortly before 1200, Magister Leoninus of the School of Notre Dame introduced strictly metrical rhythms in triple meter (see *HDM,* "Modes, Rhythmic").

12. Gutenberg's Bible was printed about 1455. Printed music (Gregorian chant) is found in liturgical books of about 1475. The earliest publication containing nothing but music is the *Odhecaton* of 1501, a collection of polyphonic compositions printed by Ottaviano dei Petrucci of Venice.

13. New edition by G. Harms (Klecken: Ugrino, 1934).

14. See the article "Organum" in *HDM.*

15. A German technical term meaning anticipating imitation, and applied to short opening passages in which the initial motive of the subsequent line of the chorale is treated in imitation.

16. The so-called Tablature of Johannes Kotter (Basle, Univ. Libr., *F IX 22*). For an almost complete edition of the keyboard dances of the sixteenth century see W. Merian, *Der Tanz in den deutschen Tabulaturbüchern* (Leipzig: Breitkopf and Härtel, 1927).

17. It is given, with the text "Belle que ma vie," in the *Orchésographie* of 1588, the most important source of information about the dances of the Renaissance, written by the canon Jehan Tabourot, who published it under the anagrammatic pseudonym of Thoinot Arbeau. New edition, in English, by C. W. Beaumont (London, 1925).

18. In the sixteenth century the term *intavolatura* (German: *Tabulatur;* French: *tablature*) was applied to all sources of keyboard and lute music, as distinguished from books containing vocal music. Today the term is used preferably for those sources of keyboard and lute music in which special systems of notation, involving letters or figures, are used.

19. Ricercar is the name for the sixteenth-century type of instrumental composition in strict imitative counterpoint, comparable to the fugue of the seventeenth and eighteenth centuries.

20. The complete works of Redford have been edited and published by Carl F. Pfatteicher (Kassel: Bärenreiter-Verlag, 1934).

21. The tempo and expression marks given with this composition are, of course, additions of the editor (Willi Apel, *Musik aus früher Zeit*).

22. New edition by J. A. Fuller Maitland and W. Barclay Squire (1894).

23. Cf. E. Pauer, *Alte Meister* (Leipzig: Breitkopf and Härtel), III, 56; Hugo Riemann, *Altmeister des Klavierspiels* (Leipzig: Steingräber-Verlag), I, 4.

24. The so-called Bauyn Manuscript, Paris, Bibl. Nat., *Vm*⁷ *674* and *675*.

25. In L. Christoph Mizler's *Neu eröffnete musikalische Bibliothek,* vol. IV, pt. 1, p. 107 (1754).

26. In order to make clear the meaning of the term "melody" as we understand it, the following remarks from Robert Schumann's "Musikalische Haus- und Lebensregeln" are quoted: " 'Melody' is the battle-cry of the dilettantes, and certainly, music without melody is no music at all. But you should know what they mean: only one easy to grasp and of pleasant rhythm. There are, however, melodies of another kind, and wherever you open Bach, Mozart, Beethoven, they look at you in a thousand different ways. Let us hope that you will soon be tired of the paltry sameness of the recent Italian operatic melodies."

27. The transcriptions by Ferruccio Busoni are outstanding, but call for a virtuoso mastery of the piano technique. Less ambitious are the transcriptions by F. Gunther (*Twenty-four Chorale Preludes by J. S. Bach*).

28. Canon is a polyphonic composition in which one voice part is imitated strictly and for its entire length in another part, or in all the parts.

29. To be accurate, the phrase "transition from polyphonic to homophonic style" should be replaced by "abandoning of polyphonic style and exclusive adoption of homophonic style." As a matter of fact, homophonic style (or a style approaching it) had been used to quite an extent throughout the Baroque period, particularly in the thorough-bass accompaniment which called for accompanying chords to be improvised as a filling in between the written-out melody and bass.

30. The question of precedence in the evolution of the "dynamic" style has become a matter of national prestige among Italian, German, and Austrian scholars. It should be pointed out that musicians like the Italian Sammartini and the Austrian Monn were active in the field alongside the German Stamitz (who actually came from Bohemia).

31. The polonaise is not a Polish folk dance, but originated, about 1600, as a court dance used for ceremonial processions. The earliest known examples of the polonaise are those found in the works of Johann Sebastian Bach (for example, in his French Suite No. VI, which is reproduced in Figure 69). Although lacking that brilliance and

rhythmic life which characterize Chopin's polonaises, they show at least one typical feature of the form, the preference for feminine endings, that is, of phrases ending on the second or third, not the first, beat of the measure.

32. The terms "classicism" and "classical" are used in this book in a restricted sense, as referring to the historical period of the "Viennese Classics": Haydn, Mozart, Beethoven, and Schubert. See the article "Classicism" in *HDM*.

33. The repeat of the exposition in the works of Haydn and Mozart is particularly significant in view of the fact that it had been discarded by some of the earlier composers such as Johann Stamitz.

34. Notable exceptions are Anton Bruckner and Paul Hindemith.

35. Two of them are of doubtful authorship.

36. Paul H. Lang, *Music in Western Civilization* (New York: W. W. Norton & Company, Inc., 1941), p. 737.

37. For more details see the article "Twelve-tone technique" in *HDM*.

38. The Boston is a type of slow waltz which was extremely popular in Europe around 1920. Its connection with the Hub of the Universe is just as obscure as that of the card game bearing the same name.

39. Ostinato designates the use of a clearly defined melodic phrase in persistent repetition, usually as a bass line (basso ostinato or ground). This method was much used in the Baroque period. See the articles "Ostinato" and "Ground" in *HDM*.

40. Hindemith's most recent work for piano, his *Ludus Tonalis* (1944), represents a twentieth-century version of the *Well-tempered Clavier*. Its study will prove equally stimulating from the point of view of present-day music and counterpoint, if indeed a distinction between these two phenomena can be made.

SOURCES

Abbreviations

DdT: Denkmäler deutscher Tonkunst, 65 volumes.
DTB: Denkmäler der Tonkunst in Bayern, 36 volumes.
DTOe: Denkmäler der Tonkunst in Oesterreich, 83 volumes.

D'ANGLEBERT, Allemande (Fig. 52). *Pièces de Clavecin, composées par J. Henry Anglebert,* edited by Marguerite Rœsgen-Champion (Paris: Publications de la Société Francaise de Musicologie, Librairie E. Droz, 1934), pp. 38–39.

ASTON, Hornepype (Fig. 37). Willi Apel, *Musik aus früher Zeit* (Mainz and Leipzig: B. Schott's Söhne [1934]), II, 5–7.

BACH, H., Erbarm Dich mein (Fig. 60). A. G. Ritter, *Zur Geschichte des Orgelspiels* (Leipzig: Max Hesse Verlag, 1884), II, 169–170.

BACH, J. C., Sonata (Fig. 85). *Zehn Klavier-Sonaten von Joh. Christian Bach,* edited by Ludwig Landshoff (Leipzig: C. F. Peters [1925]), p. 63.

BACH, J. S., French Suite No. VI (Fig. 69). *Johann Sebastian Bach's Werke* (Leipzig: Bach-Gesellschaft), XIII, pt. 2, 120–127.

BACH, J. S., In Dulci Jubilo (Fig. 70). *Johann Sebastian Bach's Orgelwerke* (Leipzig: Bach-Gesellschaft), IV, 74–75.

BACH, J. S., Prelude and Fugue (Fig. 68). *Das Wohltemperirte Klavier von Joh. Seb. Bach,* edited by Franz Kroll (Leipzig: C. F. Peters), pp. 26–29.

BACH, K. P. E., Andante (Fig. 83). *Die Preussischen Sonaten C. Ph. Em. Bachs für Klavier,* edited by Rudolph Steglich (Nagels Musik-Archiv, no. 6; Hannover: Adolph Nagel, 1927), p. 6.

BACH, W. F., Polonaise (Fig. 82). *Fugen und Polonaisen für Pianoforte von Wilh. Friedemann Bach,* edited by Walter Niemann (Leipzig: C. F. Peters, 1914), pp. 28–29.

BARTÓK, Allegro Barbaro (Fig. 131). Béla Bartók, *Allegro Barbaro* (London: Boosey and Hawkes, Ltd. [1939]).

BAUMGARTNER, Organ Composition (Fig. 19). Willi Apel, *Musik aus früher Zeit* (Mainz and Leipzig: B. Schott's Söhne [1934]), I, 4.

BEETHOVEN, Early Sonata (Fig. 90). *Drei Sonaten fürs Klavier . . . verfertiget von Ludwig van Beethoven* (Speier in Rath Bosslers Verlag, 1783).

BEETHOVEN, Sonata "Les Adieux" (Fig. 109). *Sämtliche Klaviersonaten von Ludwig van Beethoven,* edited by Heinrich Schenker (Vienna: Universal-Edition, A.G.), II, 466.

BEETHOVEN, Sonata op. 2, no. 1 (Fig. 91). *Ludwig van Beethoven's Werke. Serie 16* (Leipzig: Breitkopf and Härtel), I, 1–2.

BEETHOVEN, Sonata op. 10, no. 3 (Fig. 94). *Ludwig van Beethoven's Werke. Serie 16* (Leipzig: Breitkopf and Härtel), I, (103) 1.

BEETHOVEN, Sonata op. 28 (Figs. 95, 96). *Ludwig van Beethoven's Werke. Serie 16* (Leipzig: Breitkopf and Härtel), II, (29) 3, (30) 4, (31) 5.

BEETHOVEN, Sonata op. 49, no. 2 (Fig. 92). *Sämtliche Klaviersonaten von Ludwig van Beethoven,* edited by Heinrich Schenker (Vienna: Universal-Edition, A.G.), II, 363.

BEETHOVEN, Sonata op. 101 (Fig. 106). *Sämtliche Klaviersonaten von Ludwig van Beethoven,* edited by Heinrich Schenker (Vienna: Universal-Edition, A.G.), II, 501.

BEETHOVEN, Sonata op. 110 (Figs. 97, 98). *Sämtliche Klaviersonaten von Ludwig van Beethoven,* edited by Heinrich Schenker (Vienna: Universal-Edition, A.G.), II, 577–578.

BRAHMS, Intermezzo (Fig. 117). *Brahms Klavier-Werke,* edited by Emil von Sauer (Leipzig: C. F. Peters), II, 61–63.

BRAHMS, Sonata op. 1 (Fig. 115). *Sonata (C dur) für das Pianoforte componirt und Joseph Joachim zugeeignet von Johannes Brahms. Op. 1* (Berlin: N. Simrock), p. 3.

BUXHEIM ORGAN BOOK, Facsimile (Fig. 18). Munich, Staatsbibliothek *Mus. Ms. 3725.*

BUXHEIM ORGAN BOOK, Organ Prelude (Fig. 17). A. T. Davison and Willi Apel, *Historical Anthology of Music* (Cambridge: Harvard University Press, 1946), p. 88.

BUXTEHUDE, Durch Adams Fall (Figs. 57, 58). *Dietrich Buxtehude Orgelkompositionen,* edited by P. Spitta, new revision by Max Seiffert (Leipzig: Breitkopf and Härtel), II, pt. 4, 85–86.

BUXTEHUDE, Prelude and Fugue (Fig. 56). *Dietrich Buxtehude Orgelkompositionen,* edited by P. Spitta, new revision by Max Seiffert (Leipzig: Breitkopf and Härtel), I, pt. 1, 41–43.

BYRD, The Carman's Whistle (Fig. 38). Julius Epstein, *Alte Meisterstücke für Klavier* (Vienna: Universal-Edition), II, 4–7.

BYRD, Pavane, The Earle of Salisbury (Fig. 39). Willi Apel, *Musik aus früher Zeit* (Mainz and Leipzig: B. Schott's Söhne [1934]), II, 11.

CABEZÓN, Differencias sobra la Pavana Italiana (Fig. 29). Hermann Halbig, *Klaviertänze des 16. Jahrhunderts* (Stuttgart and Berlin: J. G. Cotta'sche Buchhandlung Nachfolger [1928]), pp. 16–18.

CABEZÓN, Versos del sexto tono (Fig. 31). A. T. Davison and Willi Apel, *Historical Anthology of Music* (Cambridge: Harvard University Press, 1946), p. 144.

CAVAZZONI, Kyrie (Fig. 32). *Girolamo Cavazzoni, Musica Sacra, Ricercari e Canzoni*, edited by Giacomo Benvenuti (Milan: Società Anonima Notari la Santa, 1919), pp. 3–4.

CHAMBONNIÈRES, Allemande la Rare (Fig. 51). *Œuvres Complètes de Chambonnières*, edited by Paul Brunold and André Tessier (Paris: Editions Maurice Senart, 1925), p. 1.

CHOPIN, A-flat Major Ballade (Figs. 104, 105). *Fr. Chopin Klavier-Werke* (Mainz and Leipzig: B. Schott's Söhne [1918]), V, 27.

CHOPIN, Nocturne op. 32, no. 1 (Fig. 107). *Friedrich Chopin's Werke*, edited by W. Bargiel, J. Brahms, A. Franchomme, F. Liszt, C. Reinecke, E. Rudorff (Leipzig: Breitkopf and Härtel [1878]), IV, 37.

CHOPIN, Nocturne op. 48, no. 1 (Fig. 103). *Friedrich Chopin's Werke*, edited by W. Bargiel, J. Brahms, A. Franchomme, F. Liszt, C. Reinecke, E. Rudorff (Leipzig: Breitkopf and Härtel [1878]), IV. 2–5.

CHOPIN, Nocturne op. 62, no. 1 (Fig. 110). *Friedrich Chopin's Werke*, edited by W. Bargiel, J. Brahms, A. Franchomme, F. Liszt, C. Reinecke, E. Rudorff (Leipzig: Breitkopf and Härtel [1878]), IV, 67.

CHOPIN, Prelude (Fig. 74). *Fr. Chopin, Préludes and Rondos*, edited by M. Raoul Pugno (Vienna: Universal-Edition), p. 3.

CLAVICHORD (Fig. 6). N. Bessaraboff, *Ancient European Musical Instruments* (Cambridge: Harvard University Press, 1941), p. 336.

COUPERIN, La Distraite (Fig. 76). *Pièces de Clavecin, composées par François Couperin*, edited by J. Brahms and F. Chrysander (London: Augener & Co., 1889), III, 307.

COUPERIN, Le Rossignol en amour (Fig. 75). *Pièces de Clavecin, composées par François Couperin*, edited by J. Brahms and F. Chrysander (London: Augener & Co., 1889), III, 241–242.

COUPERIN, Le Tic-Toc-Choc (Fig. 72). *Pièces de Clavecin, composées par François Couperin*, edited by J. Brahms and F. Chrysander (London: Augener & Co., 1889), III, 282–283.

DEBUSSY, Et la lune descend (Fig. 123). Claude Debussy, *Images; 2ᵉ Serie pour Piano seul* (Paris: A Durand & Fils, 1908).

DEBUSSY, Sarabande (Fig. 122). Claude Debussy, *Pour le Piano—Prélude –Sarabande–Toccata* (Paris: E. Fromont, 1901).

FISCHER, Prelude and Fugue (Fig. 64). *Sämtliche Werke für Klavier und Orgel von Johann Kaspar Ferdinand Fischer,* edited by Ernst V. Werra (Leipzig: Breitkopf and Härtel [1901]), p. 78.

FISCHER, Suite (Fig. 63). *Sämtliche Werke für Klavier und Orgel von Johann Kaspar Ferdinand Fischer,* edited by Ernst V. Werra (Leipzig: Breitkopf and Härtel [1901]), pp. 12–13.

FRESCOBALDI, Canzona (Fig. 47). *Hieronymus Frescobaldi, Augewählte Orgelsätze,* edited by Fr. X. Haberl (Leipzig: Breitkopf and Härtel), pp. 30–31.

FRESCOBALDI, Toccata (Fig. 45). G. Tagliapietra, *Anthologie Alter und Neuer Musik für Klavier* (Milan: G. Ricordi & Co., 1934), IV, 24–28.

FROBERGER, Lamentation (Fig. 54). *Johann Jakob Froberger's Werke für Orgel und Klavier* (Leipzig: Breitkopf and Härtel; Vienna: Artoria & Comp., 1903), II, 93–94.

FROBERGER, Suite (Fig. 53). *Johann Jakob Froberger's Werke für Orgel und Klavier* (Leipzig: Breitkopf and Härtel; Vienna: Artoria & Comp., 1903), II, 1–3.

GABRIELI, Intonazione (Fig. 34). A. T. Davison and Willi Apel, *Historical Anthology of Music* (Cambridge: Harvard University Press, 1946), p. 146.

GALUPPI, Sonata (Fig. 80). Giacomo Benvenuti, *Cembalisti Italiani del Settecento: Diciotto Sonate* (Milan: G. Ricordi e C.), p. 10.

GIBBONS, The Lord of Salisbury His Pavin (Fig. 40). *Orlando Gibbons, Complete Keyboard Works,* edited by Margaret H. Glyn (London: Stainer & Bell Ltd. [1925]), III, 4–5.

HARPSICHORD (Fig. 5). N. Bessaraboff, *Ancient European Musical Instruments* (Cambridge: Harvard University Press, 1941), p. 329.

HARPSICHORD, action (Fig. 7). N. Bessaraboff, *Ancient European Musical Instruments* (Cambridge: Harvard University Press, 1941), p. 322.

HAYDN, Sonata (Fig. 84). *Sonaten von Joseph Haydn,* edited by Louis Köhler and F. A. Roitzch (Leipzig: C. F. Peters, 1901), II, 54–58.

HINDEMITH, First Piano Sonata (Fig. 140). Paul Hindemith, *Sonaten für Klavier* (Mainz and Leipzig: B. Schott's Sohn [1936]), pp. 4–5.

HYDRAULIS, clay model (Fig. 1). *Grove's Dictionary of Music and Musicians* (3rd edition; London: Macmillan and Co., 1927), II, plate xxxvi.

ILEBORGH, Organ Prelude (Fig. 15). Willi Apel, "Early German Keyboard Music," *The Musical Quarterly,* XXIII (1937), 210.

ILEBORGH TABLATURE, FACSIMILE (Fig. 13). Curtis Institute of Music, Philadelphia.

KUHNAU, Saul Malinconico (Fig. 62). DdT, IV, 135–136.

LISZT, Étude (Fig. 114). *Franz Liszts Musikalische Werke. Serie 2* (Leipzig: Breitkopf and Härtel [1911]), II, 13.

LISZT, Second Elegy (Fig. 113). *Franz Liszts Musikalische Werke. Serie 2* (Leipzig: Breitkopf and Härtel [1927]), IX, (101) 1– (106) 6.

MENDELSSOHN, Song Without Words (Fig. 111). *Felix Mendelssohn Bartholdy's Werke,* edited by Julius Rietz. *Serie 11* (Leipzig: Breitkopf and Härtel), III, (64) 8.

MENDELSSOHN, Venetian Boatsong (Fig. 112). *Felix Mendelssohn Bartholdy's Werke,* edited by Julius Rietz. *Serie 11* (Leipzig: Breitkopf and Härtel), III, (65) 9– (66) 10.

MERULO, Toccata (Fig. 35). A. T. Davison and Willi Apel, *Historical Anthology of Music* (Cambridge: Harvard University Press, 1946), p. 168.

MOZART, Air Varié (Fig. 88). *Mozart, Variationen für Klavier zu 2 Händen,* edited by Louis Köhler and A. Ruthardt (Leipzig: C. F. Peters), p. 96.

MOZART, Sonata (Fig. 87). *Sonaten von W. A. Mozart,* edited by Louis Köhler (Leipzig: C. F. Peters), p. 76.

MOZART, Sonata in B-flat (Fig. 86). *Sonaten von W. A. Mozart,* edited by Louis Köhler (Leipzig: C. F. Peters), p. 36.

MOZART, Variations La belle Française (Fig. 89). *Mozart, Variationen für Klavier zu 2 Händen,* edited by Louis Köhler and A. Ruthardt (Leipzig: C. F. Peters), pp. 31–37.

NÖRMIGER, Der Mohren Auftzugkh (Fig. 41). Willi Apel, *Musik aus früher Zeit* (Mainz and Leipzig: B. Schott's Söhne [1934]), I, 14.

NÖRMIGER, Der Schefer Tantz (Fig. 42). Hermann Halbig, *Klaviertänze des 16. Jahrhunderts* (Stuttgart and Berlin: J. G. Cotta'sche Buchhandlung Nachfolger [1928]), p. 28.

ORGAN, from the van Eyck altar of Ghent (Fig. 4). Fogg Art Museum, Cambridge.

ORGAN, from the Obelisk of Theodosius (Fig. 2). *Grove's Dictionary of Music and Musicians* (3rd ed.; London: Macmillan and Co., 1927), III, 737.

ORGAN, from the Utrecht Psalter (Fig. 3). Houghton Library, Cambridge.

PACHELBEL, Suite (Fig. 61). DTB, vol. II, pt. 1, pp. 81–83.

PAUMANN, Mit ganczem willen (Fig. 16). Willi Apel, *Musik aus früher Zeit* (Mainz and Leipzig: B. Schott's Söhne [1934]), I, 3.

PAVANE (Fig. 27). August Halm, *Klavierübung,* II, edited by Willi Apel (Kassel: Bärenreiter-Verlag [1932]), 15.

POGLIETTI, Aria Allemagna (Fig. 55). DTOe, vol. XIII, pt. 2, pp. 13–22.

POULENC, Mouvements Perpétuels (Fig. 137). Francis Poulenc, *Mouvements Perpétuels, pour piano* (J. & W. Chester, Ltd., 1919), p. 2.

RAMEAU, Les Cyclopes (Fig. 77). *Jean-Philippe Rameau, Œuvres complètes; I: Pièces de Clavecin,* edited by C. Saint-Saëns (Paris: A. Durand et fils, 1895), pp. 54–58.

ROBERTSBRIDGE CODEX, facsimile (Fig. 9). H. E. Woolridge, *Early English Harmony* (London: Bernard Quaritch, 1897), vol. I, plate 43.

ROBERTSBRIDGE CODEX, Organ Estampie (Fig. 10). Willi Apel, *Musik aus früher Zeit* (Mainz and Leipzig: B. Schott's Söhne [1934]), II, 1.

SCARLATTI, Sonata (Fig. 78). L. Hoffman-Behrendt, *Altitalienische Klaviermusik. Acht Sonaten des Domenicho Scarlatti* (Stuttgart and Berlin: J. G. Cotta'sche Buchhandlung Nachfolger [1927]), pp. 3–5.

SCHEIDT, Wehe, Windgen, Wehe (Fig. 48). DdT, I, 51–55.

SCHLICK, Maria zart (Fig. 25). A. G. Ritter, *Zur Geschichte des Orgelspiels* (Leipzig: Max Hesse Verlag, 1884), II, 96.

SCHLICK, Salve Regina (Figs. 23, 24). A. T. Davison and Willi Apel, *Historical Anthology of Music* (Cambridge: Harvard University Press, 1946), pp. 101–102.

SCHOENBERG, Sechs kleine Klavierstücke, No. V (Fig. 127). Arnold Schönberg, *Sechs kleine Klavierstücke, Op. 19* (Vienna, Universal-Edition, A. G. [1913]), p. 7.

SCHOENBERG, Trio (Fig. 130). Arnold Schönberg, *Suite für Klavier, op. 25* (Vienna: Universal Edition, A. G. [1925]), p. 19.

SCHUBERT, Andante from a Sonata in B-flat (Fig. 99). *Sonaten von Franz Schubert,* edited by Louis Köhler and Adolf Ruthardt (Leipzig: C. F. Peters), pp. 204–209.

SCHUMANN, Davidsbündlertänze (Fig. 100). *Robert Schumann's Werke, Serie 7* (Leipzig: Breitkopf and Härtel), I, 96–119.

SCHUMANN, Grande Sonata, op. 11 (Fig. 101). *Robert Schumann's Werke, Serie 7* (Leipzig: Breitkopf and Härtel), III, 4.

SCHUMANN, Novellette (Fig. 73). *Rob. Schumann's Werke für Pianoforte,* edited by A. Dörffel and R. Schmidt (Leipzig: C. F. Peters), II, 274 .

SCHUMANN, Phantasie, op. 17 (Fig. 102). Robert Schumann, *Phantasie, Op. 17* (Leipzig: C. F. Peters).

SCRIABIN, Album Leaf (Fig. 125). A. Scriabin, *Album for the Pianoforte* (Boston: The Boston Music Company), pp. 20–21.

SCRIABIN, Prélude (Fig. 126). A Scriabin, *Cinq Préludes pour Piano, op. 74* (Moscow: P. Jurgenson [1923]), No. 3.

STRAVINSKY, Sérénade, Hymne (Fig. 135). Igor Stravinsky, *Sérénade en La, en quatre mouvements, pour piano* (Berlin: Édition Russe de Musique [1926]), pp. 3–5.

STRAVINSKY, Sonata for Two Pianos (Fig. 136). Igor Stravinsky, *Sonata for Two Pianos* (New York: Associated Music Publishers, Inc. [1945]), p. 9.

STRAVINSKY, Valse (Fig. 133). H. Autenrieth-Schleussner, *Das neue Klavierbuch* (Mainz: B. Schott's Söhne), III, 4–5.

SWEELINCK, Mein junges Leben hat ein End (Fig. 43). *Werken van Jan Pieterzn. Sweelinck,* edited by Max Seiffert ('s-Gravenhage: Martinus Nijhoff, 1894), I, 99–102.

WECK, Spanyöler Tancz (Fig. 26). Hermann Halbig, *Klaviertänze des 16. Jahrhunderts* (Stuttgart and Berlin: J. G. Cotta'sche Buchhandlung Nachfolger [1928]), pp. 5–6.

WILKIN TABLATURE (Fig. 12). Berlin, Staatsbibliothek, *Theol. quart.* 290.

INDEX

Asterisks indicate illustrations. Indication of subsequent pages (f., ff.) refers to pages with text only, disregarding those containing illustrations.

Accidentals, 33f.
Air Varié (Mozart) , *198
Alberti bass, 174
Album Leaf (Scriabin) , 282, *283
Allegro Barbaro (Bartók) , 292, *293
Allemande, 43, 93, *96, 97, *98, 100, 190
Allemande la Rare (Chambonnières) , *96
Altar of Ghent, 9, *10
Ammerbach, Nikolaus, 69
Anglebert, Jean Henri d', 97, 100; Allemande, *98
Antiphons B.M.V., 37
Anti-romanticism, 273, 297
Aria Allemagna (Poglietti) , 109, *110
Ariadne musica (Fischer) , 133f., 139
Arpichordo, 4
Ars nova, 280
Art of Fugue (J. S. Bach) , 137, 153
Aston, Hugh, 57; Hornepype, 60, *62
Atonality, 287f., 298f.

Babcock, Alpheus, 19
Bach, Heinrich, 124; Erbarm dich mein, *125
Bach, J. Christian, 19, 191f., *192, 206
Bach, J. Christoph, 124
Bach, J. Michael, 124
Bach, J. Sebastian, 37, 42, 51, 55, 68, 75, 104, 110, 136ff., 139, 153, 206ff., 295f.; French Suite No. VI, *147, 190; In Dulci Jubilo, *151, *154; Prelude and Fugue, *142, 146
Bach, K. P. E., 178ff., 183, 184, 190f.; Andante, *182
Bach, W. F., 178, 181; Polonaise, *179
Bagatellen (Beethoven) , 239
Balbastre, 19
Ballade (Chopin) , *248
Ballet Suite, 133
Baroque, Music of the, 77ff.

Baroque Organ, 6, 13, 76, 113, 118, 150
Bartók, Béla, 292; Allegro Barbaro, *293
Basse danse, 43
Baumgartner, Organ composition, *31, 32, 33, 49
Beethoven, Ludwig van, 136f., 174, 177, 206f., 239, 249; Sonatas, *177, *208, *210, *215, *217, *220, 221, *222, 224, 231, 239, 249, *250, *251
Belle Française, La (Mozart) , *200
Besard, Jean-Baptiste, 100
Beyle (Stendhal) , 25, 225
Binary form, 185f.
Binchois, 24, 32
Bitonality, 298, 300f., *302
Böhm, Georg, 110, 119
Boston, Valse (Hindemith) , 295
Bourrée, 100
Brahms, Johannes, 264ff.; Intermezzo, *269; Sonata, *267
Branle, 43
Brent, John, 18
Broadwood, John, 18
Bruckner, Anton, 224
Bruhns, Nikolaus, 110, 119
Bull, John, 61, 65, 72
Burgundian School, 24, 32, 36
Burney, 19
Busoni, Ferrucio, 281
Buxheim Organ Book, 28ff., *30, 32, 36
Buxtehude, Dietrich, 55, 110, 113, 119; Durch Adams Fall, 119, *120, 124; Prelude and Fugue, *114
Byrd, William, 61, 65; Carman's Whistle, *66; Pavane, *68
Byzantium, Organ in, 7

Cabezón, Antonio de, 45ff., 65, 117; Diferencias sobra la Pavana Italiana, *46; Versos del sexto tono, *50, 51

Cantio Belgica (Scheidt), 92
Cantus firmus, 37, 39, 50, 53
Cantus-firmus chorale, 118f.
Canzona, 35, 87, 88f., *90, 117
Canzona (Frescobaldi), *90
Capriccio, 87
Carnaval (Schumann), 238
Carman's Whistle (Byrd), *66
Carthage, Organ of, 6, *7, 10
Cavazzoni, Girolamo, 51ff., 117; Kyrie, *52
Cembalo, 17
Chambonnières, Jacques Champion de, 92ff., 97, 100; Allemande, 93, *96, 97
Character piece, 232f., 239
Chekker, 17
Chopin, Frédéric François, 158, 240ff.; Ballade, *248, *249; Nocturnes, *243, *244, *250, *251; Prelude, *159
Chorale canon, 119
Chorale fantasia, 119f.
Chorale fugue, 119, *124, 126
Chorale motet, 118
Chorale prelude, 116ff., *120, *125, 146f., *151, *153
Christofori, Bartolommeo, 18
Chromaticism, 249, 252, 299
Classicism, 184ff.
Clavecin, 17, 95
Clavicembalo, 4, 17
Clavichord, 3ff., 12ff., *13, *15
Cocteau, Jean, 292
Contrary motion, 23
Copronymos, Emperor, 7
Counterpoint, 174, *175, 297, *298
Couperin, François, 97, 101, 156ff.; La Distraite, *162, 164; Le Rossignol en amour, *160; Le Tic-Toc-Choc, *158
Couperin, Louis, 100
Courante, 43, 100
Cyclopes, Les (Rameau), 164, *165

Dance music, 23, 35, 42ff., *44, *45, 57f., *62, 65f., *68, 71f., *72, *73, 92ff., *96, 97ff., *98, 127, 133, 146, 294ff. *See also* Suite
Davidsbund, 232
Davidsbündlertänze (Schumann), 232, *233, 238
Debussy, Claude, 268, 273ff.; Et la lune descend, *278; Sarabande, *277
Development, 185, 199, 216ff.
Diferencias sobra la Pavana Italiana (Cabezón), 45, *46, 49

Dissonance, 34, 283ff., 290ff., 298
Distraite, La (F. Couperin), 161, *162
Dixit Dominus, *49, 50
Double escapement, 19
Double pedal, 28
Drei Klavierstücke (Schoenberg), 282
Dufay, Guillaume, 24, 32, 36
Dulcimer, 18
Dunstable, John, 32
Durch Adams Fall (Buxtehude), 119, *120, 124

Editorial accidentals, 33f.
Elegy, Second (Liszt), *258
Empfindsamkeit, 178
English Suites (J. S. Bach), 146
Episodes, 88
Equal temperament, 146
Érard, Sébastien, 19
Erbarm dich mein (H. Bach), *125
Eschiquier, 17
Espinette, 4
Estampie, 23f.
Et la lune descend (Debussy), 276f., *278
Etudes (Liszt), 264f., *265
Eusebius, 232
Exaquir, 17
Exposition, 185f., 221
Eyck, Jan van, 9

Fantasia, 87
Fantasia (Schumann), *see* Phantasie
Fauxbourdon, 32, 275
Fischer, J. K. F., 130ff., 139, 140; Prelude and Fugue, *136; Suite, *134
Fitzwilliam Virginal Book, 61
Flemish School, 36
Florestan, 232
French Overture (J. S. Bach), 133
French Suite (J. S. Bach), 146, *147, 190
Frescobaldi, Girolamo, 79ff., 89, 92, 109, 110; Canzona, *90; Toccata, 81, *82
Froberger, Johann Jakob, 101, 104ff.; Lamentation, *105, 107; Suite, *102
Fugue, 79, 87ff., 110, 133f., 139f., 220
Fundamentum organisandi (Paumann), 28

Gabrieli, Andrea, 53, 55; Intonazione, *54
Gabrieli, Giovanni, 53
Gagliarda, 100
Gallant style, 157
Galliard, 68

INDEX

Galuppi, Baldassare, 174; Sonata, *176
Gavotte, 100
Ghent, Altar of, 9f., *10
Gibbons, Orlando, 61, 65, 69; Pavin, *70
Gigue, 43
Goldberg Variations, 18, 76
Gothic organ, 11, 13
Grande Sonata (Schumann), 239, *240
Grazioli, 192
Greek organ, 6
Gregorian chant, 28, 37, *49, 51f., *53
Gregorian Mass IV, *53
Gundolf, Friedrich, 232

Halm, August, 207, 213
Hardulis, 7
Harmonic rhythm, 250f.
Harmony, 249f.
Harpsichord, 3ff., *12, 13ff., *14, 17f., 61, 95f.
Haydn, Josef, 174, 184ff.; Sonata, *186, 199
Hebenstreit, Pantaleon, 18
Hindemith, Paul, 34, 294ff., 302f.; Sonata, 303, *304
Hoffman, E. T. A., 230
Hoftanz, 43
Homophonic, 174, *175c, d
Honegger, Arthur, 294
Hornepype (Aston), 57, 60, *62
Hydraulic organ, 6, *7

Ileborgh, Adam, 25, 27; Organ prelude, *27, 29
Ileborgh Tablature, *26, 27
Imitation, 41ff., 51, 87, 118f.
Impressionism, 274ff., 281, 292, 297
In dulci jubilo (J. S. Bach), 150, *151, *154
Indy, Vincent d', 287
Intermezzo (Brahms), 268, *269
Intonazione (A. Gabrieli), *54
Italian Concerto (J. S. Bach), 16, 18, 153

Jack, 14
Jazz, 294f.

Krenek, Ernst, 290ff.
Krieger, Johann, 101, 124
Ktesibios, 6
Kuhnau, Johann, 124, 127ff., 138; Saul Malinconico, *131

Kyrie, 52f., *53
Kyrie (Cavazzoni), *52

Lament, 104
Lamentation (Froberger), 104, *105, 107
Landini, Francesco, 9
Liszt, Franz, 65, 240, 255ff.; Etudes, 264, *265; Second Elegy, *258
Lord of Salisbury His Pavin (Gibbons), *70
Lübeck, Vincent, 110
Luther, Martin, 117f.
Lydian mode, 33, 49

Machine music, 293f.
Magrepha, 7
Manachord, Manicordion, 4
Mannheim School, 174, 177
Maria zart (Schlick), *39, 41f., 53, 117, 118
Mazeppa (Liszt), 264, *265
Mein junges Leben (Sweelinck), *74, 76
Melodic analysis, 140f., 192f., 213f., 253
Melody chorale, 119, 126
Mendelssohn, Felix, 240, 252ff.; Song Without Words, 253, *254; Venetian Boatsong, 255, *256
Merulo, Claudio, 55ff., 81, 113; Toccata, *57
Middle Ages, Music of the, 20ff.
Middle-German School, 124ff.
Milhaud, Darius, 294
Minuet, 100, 133, 190
Missa Apostolorum (Cavazzoni), 53
Mit ganczem Willen (Paumann), 28, *29
Mohren Auftzugkh, Der (Nörmiger), *72
Monody, 78, 297
Motive, Motival technique, 193f., 199, 224f.
Moonlight Sonata (Beethoven), 212, 217, 239
Mouvements perpétuels (Poulenc), 300, *301
Mozart, W. A., 174, 181, 190, 191ff.; Air Varié, *198; La belle Française, *200; Sonatas, *193, *194
Musica ficta, 33f.
Musical Offering (J. S. Bach), 137

Nachtstück (Hindemith), 295
Nationalism, 273
Negro art, 292
Neo-classicism, 281, 297f., 302

New Music, 280ff.
Nocturne (Chopin), 243, *244, *250, *251
Nörmiger, August, 69; Der Mohren Auf-tzugkh, *72; Der Schefer Tantz, *73
North-German School, 109ff.
Novalis, 230
Novellette (Schumann), 158, *159

Obrecht, Jakob, 25, 36
Ockeghem, Jean, 24, 36
Ordre, 157
Organ, 6ff., *7, *8, *10, 18, 20
Organ chorale, 35, 113ff.
Organ composition (Baumgartner), *31, 32, 33, 49
Organetto, 9
Organ prelude (Ileborgh), *27, 29
Ornamentation, 95
Ornamented chorale, 119
Ostinato technique, 295

Pachelbel, Johann, 104, 124ff., 146; Suite, *127
Padovano, 100
Paganelli, Giuseppi, 176
Pandiatonicism, 298f., *299
Pantalon, 18
Papillons (Schumann), 238
Paradies, Pietro, 174
Paradiso degli Alberti, 9
Parallel chords, 268, *274, *275
Parallel fifths, 23
Parallel thirds and sixths, 32, 268, 274f.
Partita, 146
Pasquini, Bernardo, 130
Passacaglia, passacaille, 133, 153
Passamezzo, 43, 100
Paumann, Conrad, 28; Mit ganczem Wil-len, *29
Pavane, Pavin, 43, 45f., *68, *70
Pavane the Earl of Salisbury (Byrd), *68
Pescetti, 192
Petrone, 24
Petrouchka chord, *302
Phantasie (Schumann), 239, *241
Pierrot Lunaire (Schoenberg), 292
Pippin, King, 7
Plainte, 104
Platti, 174
Poglietti, Alessandro, 109; Aria Allemagna, *110
Polonaise, 100, 178, *179

Polonaise (W. F. Bach), *179
Polyphonic, *see* Counterpoint
Portative organ, 9
Positive organ, 9, *10
Poulenc, Francis, 294, 300; Mouvements perpétuels, *301
Pratello, 293
Praeambulum, *see* Prelude
Praetorius, Jakob, 75
Prelude, 25ff., *26, *27, 29f., *30, *54, 55, 110, 133, 158, *159, *285
Prelude and Fugue, 110, *114, 133, *136, *142, 146
Program music, 109, *110, 130, *131
Psalm tone, 49
Punctus, 24

Ragtime, 294f.
Rameau, Jean Philippe, 92, 164; Les Cyclopes, *165
Recapitulation, 185f.
Reckless counterpoint, 298
Redford, John, 56, 117
Registration, Stops, 9f., 15f.
Re di Spagna, Il, 11, 43
Reinken, Johannes, 110
Renaissance, Music of the, 35ff.
Renaissance organ, 11
Rhythm, 292
Ricercar, 35, 55, 87f., 290
Riemann, Hugo, 87
Ripresa, 100
Robertsbridge Codex, 20ff., *21, *22, 27
Rococo, 78, 156ff.
Romanticism, 101, 104, 107, 221, 230ff., 273, 281, 287, 297
Rossi, Lorenzo di, 81
Rossi, Michelangelo, 81
Rossignol en amour (F. Couperin), *160
Rousseau, Jean Jacques, 178
Rutini, Giovanni, 174

St. Marks, 55
Saltarello, 43, 100
Salve Regina (Schlick), 37f., *38, 39, 49, 117, 118
Sammartini, Giovanni, 138, 174
Sarabande, 43, 100
Sarabande (Debussy), 276, *277
Satie, Erik, 281, 295
Satire, 281, 295
Saul Malinconico (Kuhnau), *131
Scale (in organ building), 10f.

Scarlatti, Domenico, 164ff.; Sonata, *170
Scenes from Childhood (Schumann), 238
Schefer Tantz, Der (Nörmiger), *73
Scheidemann, Heinrich, 75, 110
Scheidt, Samuel, 75, 89; Wehe, Windgen, Wehe, 92, *93
Schildt, Melchior, 75
Schlick, Arnolt, 11, 32, 36f., 51, 53, 89, 117, 118; Maria zart, *39, 41f.; Salve Regina, 37, *38, 39
Schmid, Bernhard, 69
Schoenberg, Arnold, 34, 282ff.; Sechs kleine Klavierstücke, 287, *288; Trio, 290, *291
Schröter, Gottlieb, 18
Schubert, Franz, 221ff.; Andante, *225
Schumann, Robert, 158, 231ff., 266; Davidsbündlertänze, 232, *233, 238; Grande Sonata, *240; Novellette, *159; Phantasie, 239, *241
Scriabin, Alexander, 281ff.; Album Leaf, 282, *283; Prelude, *285
Sechs kleine Klavierstücke (Schoenberg), 287, *288
Second Elegy (Liszt), *258
Sérénade en La (Stravinsky), 299
Silbermann, Gottfried, 18
Sonata, 127f., 130, 164f., *170, *176, 181, *182, 184, *186, *193, *194, 207f., *208, *210, *212, *215, *217, *220, 221, *222, 224f., *225, 239, *240, 266, *267, 299, *300, 303, *304
Sonata-form, 185ff.
Sonetti di Petrarca (Liszt), 258
Song Without Words (Mendelssohn), 252ff., *254
South-German School, 109f.
Spanyöler Tancz (Weck), 43, *44
Spinetto, 4
Stamitz, Johann, 174, 177
Stendhal, see Beyle
Stops, see Registration
Stravinsky, Igor, 34, 295, 299; Sonata, *300; Valse, *296
Strauss, Richard, 281
Strozzi, Gregorio, 130
Suite, 43, 97ff., *102, 124ff., *127, 133, *134, 146, *147, 157, 294f.
Suite 1922 (Hindemith), 294f.
Sweelinck, Jan Pieterzoon, 72, 75ff., 89, 109; Mein junges Leben, *74

Tallis, Thomas, 56
Tangent, 15
Taverner, John, 56
Telemann, Georg, 138
Ternary form, 185, 239, 243
Thalberg, Sigismund, 252
Themes (in fugues and sonatas), 139f., 192f., 213ff., 224f.
Theodosius, Emperor, 7
Tic-Toc-Choc, Le (F. Couperin), *158
Tieck, 230
Timbre, 10f., 13
Toccata, 35, 55ff., *57, 81, *82, 110ff., 113
Tombeau, 104
Tonality, 283f.
Tone-poems, 231
Tone-row, 289f., *290
Trio (Schoenberg), 290, *291
Tunder, Franz, 110, 119
Twelve-tone technique, 289ff.

Upright piano, 17
Utrecht Psalter, *8

Valse (Stravinsky), 295, *296
Variations, 45ff., *46, 65ff., *66, *74, 76, 92, *93, *198, 199f., *200, 299, *300
Variation canzona, 89, *90
Venetian Boatsong (Mendelssohn), 255, *256
Venetian School, 54f.
Veracini, Francesco, 190
Versos del sexto tono (Cabezón), 49, *50, 51
Virdung, Sebastian, 18
Virginalistic music, 61
Voltaire, 19
Vocal music, 23
Vorimitation, 42

Water organ, see Hydraulis
Watteau, 156
Weck, 44; Spanyöler Tancz, *44
Weckmann, Matthias, 110
Wehe, Windgen, Wehe (Scheidt), 92, *93
Well-tempered Clavier (J. S. Bach), 4, 16, 110, 136, 139, *142, 146, 207
Whole-tone scale, *276
Wilkin tablature, 24
Winchester organ, 8f.
Wölfflin, Heinrich, 77
Wulstan, 8